MW00443819

WRITINGS OF THE ISLANDS

WRITINGS OF THE ISLANDS

Sullivan's Island and Isle of Palms

SUZANNAH SMITH MILES

CHARLESTON LONDON
the
History
PRESS

Other local history books by Suzannah Smith Miles:

The Beach
East Cooper Gazetteer
Island of History: Sullivan's Island from 1670-1860
Time and Tides on the Long Island: Isle of Palms History, Flora and Fauna
The Sewee, Island People of the Carolina Coast
Scoundrels, Heroes & the Lowcountry Outdoors
Writings of the Past
Writings of the Lowcountry

Published by The History Press
18 Percy Street
Charleston, SC 29403
866.223.5778
www.historypress.net

First published 2004

Manufactured in the United Kingdom

ISBN: 1-59629-004-8

Library of Congress CIP data applied for.

CONTENTS

This book is dedicated to the memory of Thomas, David and Paul Keegan.

Preface

M Y FAMILY MOVED TO SULLIVAN'S Island in 1958. We had been living in downtown Charleston and moving to "the island" was, in more ways than one, a drastic change. People summered on the island, certainly. But live there year round? September came and you moved back to town. In winter (pronounced as "winta-time" by islanders), life on the island was utter tranquility. With the summer people gone, the population dwindled to less than two hundred souls. The only downside: summer cottages didn't have proper heating. Why would they need it?

Ah, but my parents had caught that deliciously addictive island fever. September came and went; we didn't. Come October, my father purchased a space heater, which strained ineptly to warm our drafty, spacious rooms—rooms designed to offset heat, not retain it. There were some cold early mornings that first winter on the island. I learned to dress quickly and truly appreciate the warmth of a cup of tea.

I didn't mind. I was eleven and thrilled with my new surroundings. I had the beach practically at my doorstep. There were all the abandoned forts to explore. I was making friends, easily, and many were friends I would keep for a lifetime. It was as if I had discovered a hidden treasure and was getting to keep it all for myself.

The treasure, however, was far more valuable than simply a childhood of grand experiences. I fell in love—deeply and forever—with the island itself. In fact, I fell in love with two islands.

Like twins, Sullivan's Island and Isle of Palms have similarities, yet because each is unique, it is often difficult to characterize the islands properly. As barrier islands, both are driven by the never-ceasing pulse of the sea—what, as a five-year-old, dear departed Paul Keegan, an inveterate islander, called "the Great Atlantic Notion."

Both islands share a rare and enviable quality: a true sense of place. One soon falls under the spell of island life. I have often marveled as I watched visitors from "away" gradually unwind, adjust, and slowly begin to adopt the gentle, casual rhythm of island time—time not measured by minutes and hours, but by the rise and fall of the tide.

A respect for the history of these islands is, perhaps, a quality I absorbed simply by being an inquisitive child living in a place so abundant with historical worth. It was only much later, far into my writing career that I began to seriously research and write this history. A large majority of my "Writings of the Past" columns with the *Moultrie News* are centered around events that occurred on the two islands.

It is largely from these columns that this book is developed. I've included some new information, topics not published previously, and a brief historical overview. There are times when my history "repeats itself," so to speak, when a topic crops up more than once in different articles. And you'll find that I have a particular fondness for writing about natural disasters, particularly hurricanes.

What I think you'll discover most, however, is that these two islands hold a wealth of interesting stories that never cease to satisfy. Here is a history replete with tales of genuine excitement—of pirates and poets, sailing ships and Sewee Indians, wars and wisdom, tragedies and tenderness, and real, honest-to-God heroes.

Enjoy.

Suzannah Smith Miles
May 2004

A Brief History

Before the arrival of Europeans, the string of five barrier islands stretching from Charleston harbor to Bull's Bay were the hunting islands of coastal Indians, particularly the Sewee, a member of the Siouan linguistic group that inhabited the area between Charleston harbor and the Santee River.

There was a time when the islands were dense maritime jungles, home to wild animals such as deer, bears, foxes, wolves, wildcats, cougars, snakes of many descriptions and alligators. Such ready game made the islands favored hunting ranges for the Indians. The adjacent waters also provided a substantial marine larder, offering these early peoples a never-ceasing menu of fish, oysters, clams, conchs and other edibles.

Since the Sewee (also spelled Seewee) had given names to the other islands in this chain (Bull's Island was "Oneiscau," Capers was "Hawan" and Dewees was "Timicau"), the Sewee probably also had names for the islands we know today as Isle of Palms and Sullivan's Island. Sadly, like the Sewee themselves, these names did not survive the centuries.

It is difficult to imagine what these islands looked like during the time of the Sewee. Yet, even populated with houses, the innate character of the barrier island environment remains strikingly evident. Thin and elongated, both islands are typical coastal barrier islands—fronted by a wide beach and sand dunes, containing a thickly vegetated interior and backed by salt marsh. Today, except for the occasional alligator and the omnipresent raccoon, the islands are tamed. Tamed, that is, except for the sea.

It is the very nature of a barrier island to continuously shift and move. We may negatively term this movement as "erosion," but the constant giving and taking of the shoreline is a natural and necessary feature of a barrier island doing its job. Aptly named, the barrier island is just that—a protective line of defense against the storms and ravages of the sea. Able to constantly reshape itself by accreting or eroding with the variables of wind and water, the barrier island is able to maintain its physical integrity. Centuries pass and storms come and go yet the adaptable barrier island endures.

Inhabiting the Islands

Be It Enacted, that . . . for the better intelligence of and to any ship that hereafter may happen upon this coast, It is Resolved that a Great Gunn be mounted at some convenient place neere the River's Mouth, which, with one charge of powder at a time shall be committed to the care of Capt. Florence O'Sullivan to be fired upon the approach of any ship or ships, and that the said be conveyed to the said place, upon Tuesday, next.

—*Journals of the Grand Council*
March 30, 1674

THE ABOVE ACT, WRITTEN ONLY four years after the settlement of Charleston, resulted in the first known habitation on Sullivan's Island and, eventually, in giving the island its name. Captain Florence O'Sullivan was an Irish soldier-of-fortune who arrived with the first colonists aboard the ship *Carolina* in 1670. He held a prestigious status in the colony and was a member of the Grand Council, the Commons House of Assembly, and a deputy to the Lord Proprietor, Sir Peter Colleton. With these credentials, he was given the important position of surveyor-general.

Ah, but historical records show that O'Sullivan was more than a bit of a rascal. Early writings refer to him as "dissentious" and the *Journals of the Grand Council* are filled with attacks against his surveying abilities. John Locke, Lord Ashley Cooper's confidant and secretary, actually called O'Sullivan "an ill-natured buggerer of children," a rather nasty vernacular attack on his character. O'Sullivan was soon relieved of his duties as surveyor-general.

It was O'Sullivan's abilities as a military man that enabled him to withstand this dubious reputation and maintain a certain position in colonial affairs. With the constant threat of attack from the Spaniards at St. Augustine, the colony needed O'Sullivan's solid military experience. They also needed a suitable watchtower and warning signal in case enemy ships were sighted. Given Sullivan's Island's strategic location at the entrance to the harbor, it was ideal for the placement of such a watch. O'Sullivan was the ideal man for the job and, from then on, the island bore his name.

During the ensuing years similar lookouts were established on islands all along the coastline. On August 21, 1702, an act was passed ordering two watches established "Northward of Sullivan's Island to Sea-Wea Bay" and it is here that one of the first historical references to Isle of Palms is given, at that time called "Long Island" for its exceptional length (seven miles). The watch was to be placed on the northeast end of the island and to be kept by "two white men and 2 Indians and one canoe." The other was located on the south point of Bull's Island and overlooked Caper's Inlet.

The watchtower on Sullivan's Island soon served a dual purpose. It served as a light beacon, as well as watchtower. In essence, it became the first lighthouse on South Carolina shores. Guiding ships safely across the ever-shifting sandbars at the entrance to Charleston's harbor was of paramount importance and, consequently, harbor pilots were required. In 1691, an act provided for paid harbor pilots to work from the watch house on Sullivan's Island, with a later amendment requiring that they pay one-half of their charges "in keeping the Public Watch House on Sullivan's Island in repair."

Devoid of vegetation . . . miserable wooden tenements . . . sands whose whiteness hurts the eyes. Visitors, then called "strangers," certainly didn't think much of Sullivan's Island in its early days. In 1817, Baron Barthélemi Sernin Du Moulin de la Barthelle de Montlezun wrote, "It is to Sullivan's Island that the rich people of Charleston go in summer to breathe the good air. You may see here several numbers of houses of rather poor appearance on a bare and sandy beach, devoid of vegetation and of shade . . . on sands whose whiteness hurts the eyes, without there being one single tree in whose shade one might relax."

And his contemporary, Francis Hall, observed in 1816 that "All the inhabitants who can afford it, then fly to a barrier sand-bank in the harbour, called Sullivan's Island, containing one well, and a few pal-mettoes; Here they dwell in miserable wooden tenements, trembling in every storm, lest (as frequently happens) their hiding places should be blown from over their heads, deluged by an inundation of the sea."

Yet, to the eyes of the Lowcountry citizenry, Sullivan's Island's physical attributes offered a welcome and very necessary alternative to the hot summer months and the diseases that accompanied them. "Generous boys and gentle girls in innocent joy resorted there," wrote Caroline Gilman in the early 1800s. They "ran and shouted in careless laughter against the breeze, or mused on those thoughts which come even to childhood from the bounding sea." Up until the 1790s, Sulli-van's Island had remained largely unpopulated except by those who had business there, such as the harbor pilots and those at Fort Moult-rie. Now that the island was owned by the state of South Carolina, the state legislature could open the island to civilian habitation. After 1791, citizens were allowed to build dwellings on one-half-acre lots.

By 1806, the newspapers were filled with advertisements for summer rentals. On April 2, 1806, the *Charleston Courier* advertised: "A HOUSE containing a hall and two bed chambers, handsomely finished, adjoin-ing Capt. Payne's and fronting the beach. On the premises are several useful offices, a filtering stone, and spout to catch rain water, & . . . This House would suit a small family, or a single gentlemen, and the rent would be very moderate." Another advertisement, from the July 2, 1805 *City Gazette* read: "To be Let for the Summer Season: An elegant and commodious HOUSE on Sullivan's Island, formerly the residence of JOSEPH BLAKE, Esq.; it is now in complete order, containing eight rooms and has every necessary Out Building. This House stands on a very elevated part of the island, affords a most enchanting view of the sea and harbour of Charleston, and is perfectly safe, as the hur-ricane in September last did not in the lease injure it." Other postings, such as this one from *The Times* on July 12, 1819, were more specific in the type of inhabitants required: "A Lady and Gentleman . . . with not more than one Child, who might wish to pass the Summer, or part of the season on the Island, could have 3 or 4 rooms, part of a commodious House, which is situated in an airy situation, and either have their own establishment, or join in the family . . . in the expenses of housekeeping. Enquire of Mr. Jones, at his Hotel in Broad-street."

Transportation to and from the island was by ferry-boat (a regular packet boat), which made twice-daily runs, carrying people, goods and the mail.

As Sullivan's Island continued to grow as a summering place, its closest neighbor, Long Island, remained almost entirely undeveloped. Early maps show a few roughly drawn roadways on the island. More than likely, these were logging roads, as the island's trees were used in much of the construction that supported nearby Sullivan's Island's growth. It was still called "Long Island," an uninhabited barrier island which people frequented only on the occasional hunting or fishing excursion. It would remain uninhabited until the 1880s.

Early Coastal Watches

WHEREAS nothing can contribute more the speedy and effectual repelling of an enemy than good and quick intelligence of their approaching, which can only be had by watches, well fitted and conveniently placed, more especially along the sea coast: Be it therefore enacted . . . That the persons hereafter named shall settle watches . . . [with] such numbers of people in such places . . . and so appointed as is hereafter provided by this Act.

　　　　　　　—From *South Carolina Statutes*, an act to settle coastal watches
　　　　　　　　　　　　　　　　　　　　　　　　　　　　c. 1704

THE MAN FOR WHOM SULLIVAN'S Island was named, Captain Florence O'Sullivan, was an Irish soldier-of-fortune and one of South Carolina's original settlers. O'Sullivan was a prominent figure in the colony and a military man, a much-needed commodity in the early stages of colonization. Early documents, however, show that he was also a man of somewhat dubious character. In the *Journals of the Commons House of Assembly* and other writings of that period, O'Sullivan is consistently mentioned in negative terms.

　　"Dissentious . . . troublesome . . . Unfit . . . Exactor of unreasonable fees . . . knavish, disliked, a very ill man," was how John Locke, secretary to Lord Anthony Ashley Cooper, described O'Sullivan. He may have been good at defense, but he was apparently a troublemaker and a man disliked by almost everyone.

Still, with the constant threat of a sea invasion from the Spanish at St. Augustine, men who had military experience were vital to the colony's defense. O'Sullivan enjoyed a privileged position within the political structure of the colony. He was given a land grant which comprised most of what is now Mount Pleasant's old village section, and he had four town lots and several other sizable tracts of land on the Ashley and Cooper Rivers. Whether he actually owned the island that bears his name is unknown. In 1674, O'Sullivan was given the responsibility of a coastal watch on the island "for the better intelligence of . . . any ship that hereafter may happen upon this coast," and that, "a Great Gun be mounted at some convenient place . . . with one charge of powder . . . committed to the care of Captain Florence O'Sullivan to be fired upon the approach of any ship or ships."

During the first years of colonization, watches such as the one on Sullivan's Island were set on almost all of the remote barrier islands along the Carolina coast. These lookouts were crude affairs, roughly made wooden towers from which men could fire a cannon or light a beacon to warn of approaching vessels. Surely, these must have been very lonely outposts. Yet the men who served as watchmen were of a far different breed than the men who preferred town or plantation life.

Colonel John Barnwell (d. 1734) wrote one of the few contemporary descriptions of these watchmen. Barnwell was in Carolina by 1701 and settled in the Port Royal Sound region where he established a plantation called "Doctors." He was both an Indian agent and an Indian fighter, earning the sobriquet "Tuscarora Jack" for his success against the warring Tuscarora Indians in North Carolina. Luckily for historians, Barnwell kept a journal. In it he described the coastal watchmen: "These Scoutmen are a wild Idle people & Continually Sotting if they can gett any Rum for Trust or money. Yet they are greatly usefull if well & Tenderly managed. . . . Their Chiefest Imploy is to hunt the forest or fish, So there is Scarce One of Them but understands the Hoe, the Axe, the Saw, as well as their Gun and Oar. . . . Being Every One in Debt, and having no Dependance on anything in this province, are ready for the Rum on the least disguise, So you may now Guess what hopefull fellows I have to deal with."

The watchmen's fondness for rum notwithstanding, more than once they raised the alarm to warn settlers of approaching hostile forces or Indians on the warpath. Watches were established on the northernmost point of Bull's Island and, similarly, on the north end of Isle of Palms, both manned by white men and Sewee Indians. South of Charleston harbor, coastal watches were put into place all along the southern coast. There was a watch at Folly Island, one on Kiawah Island, and Thomas Grimball was responsible for an outpost on appropriately named Watch Island, described as lying "to the southward of North Edisto River's mouth." This was probably present-day Botany Bay Island. Each of these watches was manned with the help of either the Kiawah or Bohicket Indians.

Traveling to and from these outposts was accomplished by boat and the most common type was a large canoe similar to that of the Indian dugout canoe. These were built from cypress or cedar logs, hewn so that they were flat on the sides and came to a point at bow and stern. Some were rather large affairs and a ten-oared canoe probably had a length of about thirty-five feet and a beam of about six feet.

In 1725, an act for establishing a ferry across Pon Pon (Edisto) River also appointed eight watchmen for that area, a region still recovering from the horrors of the Yemassee Indian War. The act gives a good description of what a watchman, also called a scout, needed in order to do his job. The act stated that "each of the scouts shall find his own horse and accoutrements, and provisions for himself and horse; and be armed with a gun, a pistol, and cutlass or hatchet, powder-horn, with at least a quarter of a pound of powder, and cartouch box, with twelve charges." They were paid seven pounds, ten shillings per month and were to serve for a year.

Interestingly, this act also provides us with one of the first historical references to the use of a guard dog in Carolina. "And to prevent the said scouts from being surprised by Indians, by day or by night, and for the better discovering and finding out where the said Indians hide and lurk . . . every one of the said eight scouts shall find and provide a large mastiff or mungrel bred dog, to go constantly along with them in their scouting."

Given the disagreeable dispositions of the watchmen (and certainly Florence O'Sullivan), one supposes that only a dog could put up with their headstrong ways. Despite their contrariness and understandable attachment to strong drink, they were some of our most able frontiersmen. With a dog, a gun, some rum, an Indian companion and a crude hut on a forlorn beach, they stood watch. Their names are now lost to history, but their vigilance helped the Carolina settlement succeed.

Crossing the Bar

THERE IS SOMETHING EVOCATIVE ABOUT foggy, January mornings and a walk on the beach. With the fog so thick you can't see past the third line of waves, enveloped in what some might term the original wet blanket, the world is narrowed to the small, white, protected space of your vision. The only sounds you hear are the muffled surf and, in the distance, the echoed booming of brooding fog horns, the language of unseen ships making their way in and out of the harbor.

Even with the technological advancements of radar, sonar and satellite-based directional systems, modern ships still rely on the voices of their foghorns to warn each other of their passage. It is an ancient language, one that hearkens back to the earliest days of sail. It is also a critical language, for even with Charleston's clearly marked, well-dredged channel through the jetties, dense fog requires the use of the horn as an extra guarantee for passing safely "across the bar."

Crossing the bar. It wasn't until the jetties were built in the late 1800s, establishing one straight, deep channel entrance, that it became reasonably easy for ships to come in or out of Charleston's harbor. Prior to this, crossing the bar was a dangerous process and, in the days of sail, sometimes impossible if the wind was blowing in the wrong direction. Complicating matters further, there were several different channels leading into the harbor, inhibited by an ever-changing line of sand bars stretching from Sullivan's Island to Morris Island, shifting as often as the tides.

Almost from the beginning of Charleston's settlement, steps were taken to help ensure a vessel's safe passage through this dangerous maze of shallows and sand bars. Strategically located at the mouth of the harbor, Sullivan's Island was the base of operations for such work. In 1690, an act was passed providing monies for three men to be "constantly employed in keeping a watch on Sullivan's Island" and for keeping beacons and fires lit to mark the channel entrance. It was also in 1690 that the first act for the "Settling of Pilotage" was passed, with Captain John Cock, Captain William Privett and Mr. William Bradley paid to act as pilots to safely guide every ship across the bar. These men were some of the earliest residents of the island, living what must have been a lonely existence in a watch house on the island. In those early days, it was probably the *only* house on the island.

By the 1720s, with Charles Town growing by leaps and bounds, a tremendous number of ships arrived almost daily. Piloting had become a vitally necessary and sought-after profession. In 1723, pilots John Hogg, Jonathan Collins, John Smith and John Watson were "obliged to keep a sufficient number of good decked boats, well-fitted," along with "proper canoes and boat*s*" available to row out to sea whenever a ship approached. Each boat was to be manned with "one good and able person," as well as the pilot and his apprentice or servant. These boats, propelled by oar and sail, were ordered by an act of the assembly to be kept on Sullivan's Island and every day they were to "go over the Bar, on the purpose to discover and go on board any ship or vessel intending for this port."

Even with a pilot on board, safe passage was not guaranteed. Early newspapers regularly reported news of vessels going aground in the attempt to cross the bar. The March 5, 1753 *Gazette* reported, "The Snow Hereford, Capt Peard, of and for Bristol, with a valuable Cargo, attempted to get out, the wind being very high, carried away her Fore-top mast, and was drove ashore." Luckily, the next morning she was "got off again, without Damage to her Hull or Cargo." The ship "*Good-Intent*, of and from Falmouth for this Port, John Lewis Master," was not so lucky, according to a report in the March 31, 1759 *Gazette*. While attempting to come in at the Swash Channel near Drunken Dick shoals, she "unfortunately got ashore upon the Northmost Breakers, and the next Morning bilged: Sunday noon, the Wind shifting suddenly to ENE from SW . . . and blowing excessive hard, no Attempts could be made to save any Thing belonging to her. She is since beat to Pieces, and even the Letters that came in her are lost, except one Parcel that drove upon Cumming's Island. The People however we all saved."

In 1832, the bar claimed certain fame via the artist and naturalist, John James Audubon. Audubon lost an entire barrel of bird skins packed in rum when the barrel was washed overboard in a sudden gale as the ship he was on, the *Nimrod* (whose master was Captain N.L. Coste), was attempting to cross the bar. Happily for the cause of art, Coste was able to salvage another barrel containing herons, cormorants and two redheaded vultures.

Not all experiences concerning the Charleston bar were marred by tragedy. By the 1840s, harbor steamers were offering regular evening cruises "to the bar"—with music, to boot. "EXCURSION TO THE BAR," ran the headline of an advertisement in the May 20, 1848 *Mercury*. "The Splendid Steam Packet METAMORA will go on an Excursion this Afternoon . . . leaving Union wharves at 4:00 and Boyce & Co. before 5—will accompany the steamship SOUTHERNER to the Bar and return at sunset. Fare 50 cents. Children half price. NB. The Cadet Band is engaged, and refreshments will be provided."

Certainly, the building of the jetties and the creation of one, single channel has made crossing the bar a much easier endeavor for modern vessels. No longer dependent on the vagaries of the wind, ships now steam headlong into the harbor (more or less) according to longshoremen's schedules, not Mother Nature's. But harbor pilots are as necessary now as they were in 1690, and no ship can enter or leave this port without a pilot on board.

As I write this, even at midday the fog is thickening, blanketing my back yard in a soft, white haze. Since I don't live far from the harbor, I can hear the deep, mournful voice of a ship's foghorn as it comes into the harbor and passes by Rebellion Roads. In three hundred-plus years, one wonders how many ships have gone before it. A hundred thousand? A million? Whichever, like countless vessels before it, guided by a harbor pilot, it is a ship that has safely crossed the bar.

Pirates

DURING WHAT WAS CALLED THE golden age of piracy (from about 1680 until about 1720) sailing the high seas was risky business. From Africa to North America, from South America to the Caribbean Sea, pirates preyed on civilian vessels with alarming regularity. Charleston and the Carolina coast were well known to the toughest of these toughs, including such nefarious characters as Calico Jack Rackam, Stede Bonnet, and the most barbaric of them all, Blackbeard.

These were *not* nice people. They were ruthless highwaymen of the sea and their brutalities make the current trend toward violence seem tame. Theirs was a rather easy set of counter-ethics, and cold-blooded murder was the least of their offenses. They robbed, plundered, bludgeoned, axed and blunderbussed their way onto passing vessels with a cruel glee, sometimes killing those on board just for the sheer "fun" of it. The rules were simple. If they wanted something, they took it by force. If they didn't like someone, they threw him overboard. Justice—at least pirate style—was swift and often brutal. For instance, one penalty for talking too much was to sew a man's lips shut with a sailing needle.

Of course, pirates lived during a rather low period in the history of man's social consciousness, a time of gross social inequities, when there were only two classes of people—the rich and the poor—and the poor could be truly downtrodden. It was a time when children were often put to work by the age of seven, when public executions were ghoulishly enjoyed as an excuse for feasting and revelry. A time when castles and gaols (jails) had torture chambers complete with thumbscrews and "the rack." Even in Charles Town, a public whipping was an accepted punishment for various crimes, with miscreants tied to "the usual tree" and lashed accordingly.

If you were a young man without money or position, a sailor's life on a merchant ship or with the Royal Navy was an option. Still, your salary was not much more than one pound a month, your rations were thin, and God-help-you if you were unlucky enough to find yourself on a ship captained by a sadist. Your life aboard ship might be an unholy hell of brutal floggings, keel haulings and beatings. In 1704, one account tells of a sea captain ordering a sailor to be flogged 600 times with an inch-thick tarred rope. The account doesn't tell whether the sailor lived or not.

Piracy, on the other hand, offered an opportunity for easy money and a remarkable amount of freedom. In fact, life aboard a pirate ship was surprisingly democratic. Although most vessels had the usual captain and sub-officers, decisions did not lay solely with the officers, but were made by the entire crew, either by a show of hands or, in the case of a "criminal" offense, by a trial. It was, in a way, an orderly form of anarchy-cum-democracy. They even had a crude set of written articles or rules, which a pirate joining into a crew had to sign, swearing over a Bible (or an ax) to obey to the death. But the rules were vastly different from those of the regular world. Article One, for instance, stated: "Every man shall have an equal vote in affairs of moment. He shall have an equal title to the fresh provisions or strong liquors at any time seized, and shall use them at pleasure unless a scarcity may make it necessary for the common good that a retrenchment may be voted."

To say that they were prodigious drinkers is an understatement. It was one thing to have your ship attacked by a band of cutthroats, literally armed to the teeth with sabers, cutlasses, muskets and pistols. It was quite another when this nasty band of marauders were insanely drunk. Sheer chaos could follow, as one sea captain wrote after pirates boarded his ship. They "hoisted upon Deck a great many half hogsheads of Claret and French Brandy; knock'd their Heads out, and dipp'd Canns and Bowls into them to drink out of: And in their Wantonness threw full Buckets upon one another. And in the evening washed the Decks with what remained in the Casks. As to bottled Liquor, they would not give themselves the trouble of drawing the Cork out, but nick'd the Bottles, as they called it, that is struck their necks off with a Cutlace." They then took all the livestock on board—geese, turkeys, chickens and ducks—and with no preparation, put them into a boiling cauldron along with a few Westphalian hams and a pregnant sow.

Unimaginable wealth could be had through pirate plunder. Loot not only included luxury goods such as gold, silver, precious gems and money, but there were also valuable commodities in the merchant vessels plying the trade routes between Europe and the Americas. And, despite the laws against trading with pirates, in some colonial cities (Charleston included), such items easily found their way onto a black market, condoned by officials who turned a blind eye to the process. For a time, trading with pirates was a generally accepted practice in Charleston, often the only way hard currency found its way into the colonial port or that some goods could be smuggled out. The trade may have been illegal, but it was a way to circumvent the restrictions and trade monopolies set by the Navigation Acts. And, of course, it was also helping some people get rich.

It wasn't until about 1715, when pirates like Stede Bonnet and Blackbeard began getting over-greedy and stalking the same ports with which they were trading, that the colonial government decided it had to do something about the pirates. Charleston, once a haven for pirates, now played a key role in the process of eliminating these scourges of the sea.

"Such a day," wrote Blackbeard in his journal. "Rum all out:—Our Company somewhat sober: Rogues a plotting . . . so I look'd Sharp for a Prize." He apparently didn't have to look far, for the following journal entry reads, "took one, with a great deal of Liquor on board, so kept the Company hot, damn'd hot, then all Things went well again."

During the summer of 1718, Blackbeard and Stede Bonnet, now sailing separately, began a reign of terror that stretched the entire Atlantic seaboard. Bonnet, sailing on the *Royal James* under his flag—a black field with a skull head centered over a bleached thighbone— was taking vessels from Delaware to the Carolinas. Blackbeard was scourging the Virginia and North Carolina coasts, the *Queen Ann's Revenge* sailing under his own fearsome flag, a devilish skeleton holding a glass (presumably of rum) in one hand and the other holding an arrow, aimed and ready to pierce a heart.

Both were ruthlessly brazen and extremely successful in capturing vessels—so much so, that finally, despite years of "friendly" relations and illegal trading with pirates, the authorities were forced to take measures. Spearheading the move to halt Blackbeard was Governor Alexander Spotswood of Virginia, who put Lieutenant Robert Maynard in command of an expedition to go after Blackbeard. At about the same time, Governor Nathaniel Johnson of South Carolina gave Colonel William Rhett the task of going after Bonnet.

Rhett was one of Charles Town's most prominent citizens and, certainly, the city's leading military man. In 1706, he had led the expedition that successfully routed a fleet of French-Spanish vessels planning to invade the town and was already a hero for his role in that affair. Now he put his military acumen to work again, equipping two sloops, the *Henry* with eight guns and seventy men, and the *Sea Nymph* with eight guns and sixty men, for war. Upon learning that Bonnet was at Cape Fear, where his ship was undergoing repairs, Rhett sailed after Bonnet on September 14, 1718.

On September 26, Rhett found Bonnet and the *Royal James* careened on a sandbar up the Cape Fear River. Attempting to take advantage of Bonnet's vulnerable position, Rhett went after him but his own ship also ran aground in the shallow waters of the river. Both hard aground, the two ships waited the night and the tides.

At dawn, with the *Royal James* afloat, Bonnet attempted to sail past Rhett's two vessels, which were still aground. But the same rising tide also freed Rhett's ships. They began to close in on the *Royal James*, forcing her into the shallows where she went aground again. Rhett followed, and once again, *his* vessels went aground, but this time, within firing range. For six hours a terrific battle ensued between the two grounded ships. Finally, with the rising tide, Rhett, aboard the *Henry*, closed in and took Bonnet and the *Royal James*.

Bonnet was brought back to Charles Town and his crew was imprisoned in the Guard House at the Half-Moon Bastion at the foot of Broad Street (now the site of the Old Exchange Building). As a gentleman, however, Bonnet was allowed to stay in one of the marshal's homes, under guard. Two of his crewmen were also with him, having agreed to turn King's evidence against the others.

Somehow, on October 15, Bonnet escaped. Dressed in women's clothing, he and his sailing master, David Heriot, slipped out of the harbor on a small sailboat. Their purpose was to hook up with another pirate, Christopher Moody, who was purportedly anchored offshore.

Hindered by a strong northeast wind, Bonnet got only as far as Sullivan's Island. Here, he hid in the myrtles and underbrush for about ten days before he was captured by William Rhett. For Bonnet this time there was no escape. After a speedy trial, Bonnet and twenty-nine of his crew were sentenced to death. Stede Bonnet, the so-called "Gentleman" pirate, was hanged on December 10, 1718, at White Point (now the Battery). His body remained hanging as a lesson to others who might consider pirating, and only after some days was his body buried ignominiously beneath the low water mark.

Blackbeard had already met his own nemesis. On November 22, 1718, Lieutenant Maynard had encountered Blackbeard near the island of Ocracoke off North Carolina's coast. Drunk, insolent and completely assured that he would win, Blackbeard attacked Maynard's vessels with one savage broadside after another, eventually coming alongside Maynard's sloop and boarding her. The two crews met in vicious hand-to-hand combat, with Maynard facing Blackbeard himself. The two simultaneously fired their pistols. Blackbeard's shot missed, but Maynard's found its mark. Incredibly, the pirate was unfazed. He lashed at Maynard with his cutlass, breaking Maynard's own cutlass in two. Just as he was about to finish Maynard off, one of Maynard's seamen slashed Blackbeard across the throat. Still, the pirate fought on, roaring and spurting blood, while others were slashing and shooting at him. Blackbeard had grabbed and cocked another pistol and was ready to fire again when, like a tree in the forest, he slowly toppled over, dead. It had taken an arsenal to kill the larger-than-life pirate. Upon inspection, his corpse had twenty-five wounds, five from pistol shots. Maynard ordered Blackbeard's head removed and placed on the bowsprit. His body was tossed overboard for the sharks.

The demise of these two well-known pirates heralded the end of the so-called "golden age" of piracy. One by one, the pirates who had ravaged the Atlantic and Caribbean oceans—Captain Kidd, Christopher Moody, Calico Jack Rackam, the "Lady Pirate" Anne Bonney and others—met similar fates. Their savage runs on trading vessels had been extremely profitable. Had they wished, they could have taken the paroles offered to them and retired with lavish wealth. But for whatever reason bad people do bad things, such respectability was anathema to the pirate; a fight to the death was more his style. For Blackbeard and Bonnet, that is exactly what they got.

The Pest House

THE YEAR IS 1706. CHARLES Town is in the grip of a deadly epidemic of yellow fever and almost every man, woman and child is sick. Many have died and the mortality rate keeps climbing. The few doctors in the colony barely understand the disease (also known as Black Vomit) and their treatments are largely unsuccessful. Then, just when it looks like it can't get any worse, the town is awakened by the cry that just outside the bar, a fleet of armed, hostile ships—an expedition from St. Augustine of French and Spanish soldiers—are planning to invade and take the town. Governor Nathaniel Johnson calls out the militia, but with so many of the inhabitants affected by the fever, finding able-bodied men poses a serious problem. A report later sent to London stated that "sickness raged in Charles Towne and had swept away great numbers of our men . . . and that upon the account of the sickness the Country Planters . . . [were] unwilling to come to defend the town." Luckily, enough men came to the city's defense. With the help of the Indians, the Spanish-French invasion was routed. Still, 140 people died in the yellow fever epidemic.

Disease was becoming the colony's most feared enemy. It had become increasingly evident that the source of epidemics was from the outside. Quarantine was the answer and in 1707, an act was passed providing for the building of a brick lazaretto, more commonly called a "pest house," on Sullivan's Island. It was to be used as a place to quarantine anyone coming into the colony found to be carrying a disease.

Pest House. It is a dismal name and it had to be a dismal spot. The first pest house was a small brick building, only 30- by 10-feet in size, and one can only imagine the wretched living conditions inside. Certainly, it was no hospital in the modern sense of the word. Its exact location is unclear. It is shown on early maps as being generally between Fort Moultrie and the Point.

There are scant records concerning the pest house until the 1740s. Following a boom in the importation of African slaves to provide labor for the ever-increasing number of Lowcountry rice plantations, fears mounted that the shipments of slaves were also bringing disease. For a time, the importation of slaves was forbidden by law. It was discovered that during this lull, the frequency of disease was, in fact, greatly reduced. Thus, on May 29, 1744, an act was passed "for the further preventing of the Spreading of Contagious or Malignant Distempers in the Province," which read, in part: "BE IT ENACTED, that no ship or vessel . . . shall arrive or come into this province over the bar of the harbour into Charlestown, with Negroes from the coasts of Africa or elsewhere . . . before all Negroes imported or brought in such ship or vessel shall have been landed and put on shore on Sullivan's Island. . . and there shall have remained for the space of ten days."

The act also called for the building of a new, "more commodious," pest house, but considering a 1747 notation in the *Journals of the Commons House of the Assembly*, the place was still a hellhole. The *Journals* describe the pest house as only including four rooms of brickwork, "without lining, ceiling or windows . . . too airy to afford much shelter to the sick."

Without question, the pest house is one of the most important and least studied aspects of South Carolina history, particularly black history. For decades, every slave imported into the colony, sick or not, was quarantined at the pest house. The first soil they touched after leaving Africa was the sand of Sullivan's Island. Imagine what it must have been like for these poor souls. After spending months at sea, they arrived scared, unknowing of what the future held and, in many cases, sick.

They must have found at least some relief when they finally stepped ashore and felt those first soothing, southerly breezes—the same "salubrious" air that eventually made the island famous as a resort.

Early descriptions paint a vivid portrait of what the slaves experienced during their arrival to America. Henry Laurens was a leading merchant in the traffic of African slaves (he would later denounce the practice of slavery and attempt to free his own slaves), and in a letter written in January 1756, he wrote: "our Pest House where the Slaves are to be placed during their Quarantine is in good order & they have a plenty of Wood at hand so that we hope the Cloathing they have will be sufficient But Captain Moses informs us he was oblig'd to put their Cloaths on a few days after they left Barbados to preserve them from the Water that came down through the Deck." Visitor Peletiah Webster visited the island in 1765 and noted in his journal, "Went with Mr. Liston [probably Thomas Liston, of the firm of Middleton, Liston & Hope, merchants in wines, hardware and slaves] . . . to Sullivan's Island where were 2 or 300 Negroes performing quarantine with the small pox . . . there is a pest-house here with pretty good conveniences . . . the most moving sight was a poor white man performing quarantine alone in a boat at anchor ten rods from shore with an awning & pretty poor accommodations."

One of the most harrowing experiences for the inhabitants of the pest house came with the hurricane of 1752. It was one of the worst hurricanes ever to hit the coast and the *South-Carolina Gazette* reported: "At Sullivan's Island, the pest-house was carried away, and of 15 people who were there 9 are lost, the rest saved themselves by adhering strongly to some of the rafters of the house when it fell, upon which they were driven some miles beyond the island, to Hobcaw."

Not all inhabitants of the pest house were slaves. In 1772, immigrants from a ship from Belfast, Ireland, were quarantined at the pest house, thus sparing the colony from an epidemic. In 1783, laws were passed which not only called for the quarantine of people, but which also ordered all cargo imported from disease-prone areas such as the Mediterranean to be "landed at the warehouse so erected on Sullivan's Island, and there be aired; and kept exposed to the air for not less than forty days, and until it shall be thought such infection contained in such cargo shall be got rid of."

Because of the continued prevalence of disease, the pest house remained a sad necessity. Still, conditions there were so deplorable that in 1770 the *South-Carolina Gazette* wrote, "if the Pest House on Sullivan's Island was made tight, warm, comfortable . . . and if some proper person was appointed constantly to reside on the Island . . . who would say, we wanted common Humanity?"

The pest house remained on Sullivan's Island until the 1790s, just before Moultrieville was incorporated, when it was relocated to Morris Island. The building was modified into one of the island's first churches, Grace Episcopal Church.

Today, all traces of the pest house are gone (Grace Church was destroyed during the Civil War), and it is difficult to imagine the lower end of Sullivan's Island, as peaceful and picturesque a spot as one can find in America, as being the same place on which the pest house stood. Where thousands of people—both black and white—were quarantined. Undoubtedly, many died, buried in a potter's field, long lost to the shifting sands and the sea.

It is something to remember, however, as we enjoy the freedoms and luxuries which today's life affords us. There were times in history when life held a darker side and even laws passed for the common good brought into being such extremes as the pest house. For almost a century, our beautiful and beloved Sullivan's Island wasn't known as a place for carefree days with children's laughter heard on the beach. For the thousands who performed their required quarantine at the pest house, it was a place where sorrow and bondage met hand in hand.

The Islands During
the Revolution

"I LOST SO MUCH SLEEP last Night my Dear Sister, by a swarm of musquitos which have quarter'd themselves on this unfortunate Island," wrote American Thomas Pinckney from Fort Sullivan in 1776, "that I am perforce Constrained to send for a Pavilion. If you send the White one which is Venerable for its Antiquity be kind enough to have the holes in it mended before it leaves the house."

Meanwhile, across Breach Inlet at the British encampment on Long Island, Englishman John Falconer was writing his brother, complaining of similar afflictions.

"We have lived on nothing but salt pork and pease," he wrote. "We sleep on the seashore, nothing to shelter us from the rains but our coats, or a miserable paltry blanket. There is nothing that grows on this paltry island, it being a mere sandbank and a few bushes which harbor millions of 'musketoes,' a great plague that not could be worse than hell itself. The oldest of our officers can not remember of ever undergoing hardships such as we have had since our arrival here."

Mosquitoes notwithstanding, the advent of the Revolutionary War made Sullivan's Island's position at the harbor entrance keenly important. The Americans knew an advance from the British by sea was expected and acted accordingly, deciding to erect a suitable fortification on the island at the mouth of the harbor. The responsibility of doing so was given to then-Colonel William Moultrie, a Lowcountry planter who had distinguished himself during the Cherokee Wars a decade earlier.

It was a daunting task, one accomplished in an impossibly short amount of time and on a site which, in his memoirs, Moultrie later described as being "quite a wilderness," with "a thick deep swamp where the fort stands, covered with live oak, myrtle and palmetto trees."

Moultrie set his men to work using the materials available, sand and palmetto logs. To General Charles Lee, then commander of American forces, the fort was entirely unsuitable, one he termed a "slaughter pen" and insisted be given up. Moultrie held his ground. And when the time came, the new "Fort Sullivan" would hold as well. The fibrous palmetto logs soaked up the British cannonballs like sponges. Despite the odds, which were considerable, the Americans won.

The Battle of Fort Sullivan occurred on June 28, 1776, one week prior to the Declaration of Independence. Moultrie's remarkable effort would go down in history as one of the great David versus Goliath defeats of the American Revolution. The British, though they greatly outnumbered the Americans in both troops and weaponry, were soundly defeated. This victory kept the British from attacking Charleston for another four years. Fort Sullivan was renamed in William Moultrie's honor and the man himself was given the rank of General.

By 1780, however, the tide had turned toward the British. While British forces began amassing on the city from the south and the west, British Admiral Mariot Arbuthnot was holding a fleet of warships offshore in readiness to attack. They did so on the morning of April 7, 1780.

For forty-two days, the British poured shot and shell on Charleston from land and sea. On the morning of May 7, Fort Moultrie was given up, taken by a detachment from the USS *Richmond*. On May 12, the city surrendered.

Under British occupation, Fort Moultrie was known as "Fort Arbuthnot" for two years. Following the Battle of Yorktown, and their ultimate defeat, the British evacuated Charleston in December 1782.

"It was a grand sight to see the enemy's fleet (upwards of three hundred sail) . . . ready to depart," wrote Moultrie, adding, "It was an ample reward for the triumphant soldier."

Indeed. Since the year after the Battle of Fort Sullivan, Moultrie's stunning victory over the British at Fort Sullivan has been commemorated each June 28 with "Carolina Day." Church bells peal. Parades, speeches and reenactments herald the occasion. Three hundred years later, the brave, courageous quest for American liberties, exemplified on the shores of Sullivan's Island, is still remembered while citizens proudly wave the flag of the state of South Carolina—a banner showing a single palmetto tree on a field of blue.

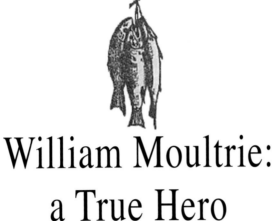

William Moultrie: a True Hero

Heroes. Today, they come packaged (sadly, that's the correct word) in the glitzy guise of rock stars and football players. They are famous, yes, but heroes?

No. Not by a long shot, especially when you measure them by the standards of a *real* hero. And without question, one of the greatest heroes to come out of the Revolutionary period was General William Moultrie.

It wasn't only that he was a great leader of men or that his garrison at Fort Sullivan so successfully routed the British fleet in June 1776. It wasn't because he served two terms as governor of South Carolina. Moultrie was also an affable, generous, openhearted gentleman whom people instantly liked and respected. One contemporary called him a man of "quiet mind and steadfast opinion." And given the choice between freedom from imprisonment (he was given a generous offer by the British to turn traitor) and the continued fight for the freedom of his country, he heroically stood behind his beliefs and the patriot cause.

William Moultrie was born in Charleston on November 23, 1730. He was the second son of Dr. John Moultrie and Lucretia Cooper, and descended from an ancient Scottish family whose name was variously spelled as Multrarre, Moultray, and finally, Moultrie. Following a family tradition, his father was educated at Edinburgh as a physician and then immigrated to Charleston around 1728 to become one of the first doctors in this town.

Little is known about William Moultrie's childhood. One can only imagine the Charles Town he knew as a boy. It was a much smaller city than it is now. The northern boundary stopped at Market Street (which was then a creek) and the tip of the peninsula was still a "white point" of oyster shells and marsh where the only building was a fortification, or "battery," erected at the very tip. Surely, he knew the cobblestoned streets and alleys of the old walled city well. Like other boys of his social station, he was probably schooled at home by a tutor and, by the time he was in his early teens, would have been well versed in the classics, able to read both Greek and Latin, and accomplished in mathematics. He probably attended one of the many dancing schools popular at that time, learning the intricacies of the minuet and waltz and likely took classes from a fencing master in the art of swordsmanship.

He had five brothers and sisters. His older brother, John, followed family tradition and was sent to Edinburgh to study medicine. His younger siblings were James, Thomas, Alexander and Cecelia, each born two years apart.

In 1751, Moultrie began his long public career—a career that spanned over forty years. He served on the Royal Assembly eleven times. He was a member of the first and second Provincial Congresses and elected to the General Assembly six times. This stellar political career culminated with his first election as governor in 1785. He was again elected governor in 1792. In 1796, forced by ill health to retire to his plantation Windsor Hill on the Ashley River, Moultrie's long public service career ended.

Paralleling his career in public office was a truly distinguished military career. It began in 1759 when, as aide-de-camp to Governor William Henry Lyttleton, Moultrie accompanied the governor to the Upcountry to fight in the Cherokee Indian war. The following year he was a captain in Colonel Thomas Middleton's Provincial Regiment and participated in the Cherokee Expedition of 1760–1761. By 1774, Moultrie had advanced to the rank of colonel in the militia. When the Revolution broke out he was given the command of the Second South Carolina Regiment of Foot. It was this "Colonel Moultrie" who was given the task of building the fortification on Sullivan's Island, then known as Fort Sullivan. Here, on June 28, 1776, his small and outgunned garrison successfully routed the British Navy under Admiral Peter Parker as they attempted to capture Charleston. The state named the fort on the island in Moultrie's honor, and he received the official thanks of the Continental Congress for his gallant conduct.

In September 1776, Moultrie's regiment became a part of the Continental Line and he was promoted to brigadier general. In February 1779, his command defeated the British at the Battle of Port Royal Island and then, in May, thwarted their drive on Charleston. When the city eventually fell in 1780, Moultrie, who was second in command of Charleston's defenses, was taken prisoner and paroled to the barracks at Haddrell's Point. He was later sent to Philadelphia and finally, in 1782, he was exchanged for General John Burgoyne. Promoted to major general, Moultrie returned to active duty and served until the end of the war.

Like many other families of that era, Moultrie's own family was torn by the politics of the time. His older brother, John, remained faithful to the Tory side, and during the war served as lieutenant governor of the Royal Province of Eastern Florida. Moultrie's younger brothers fought on the patriot side. Thomas, a captain, was killed during the siege of Charleston. Alexander commanded a militia company, the Musketeers, and eventually became the first attorney general of the Independent State of South Carolina in March 1776.

It was while he was a prisoner of war that Moultrie was given a generous offer from his long-time friend and now foe, Lord Charles Montague, to turn traitor. Lord Montague had been South Carolina's royal governor in 1776. Basically, Montague offered Moultrie the opportunity to join him in Jamaica, where Moultrie would be given a command. Wrote Montague, "You have now fought bravely in the cause of the country for many years and, in my opinion, fulfilled the duty every individual owes to it. You have had your share of hardships and difficulties and if the contest is still to be continued, younger hands should now take the toil from you. You have now a fair opening of quitting the service with honor and reputation to yourself by going to Jamaica with me. The world will readily attribute it to the known friendship that has subsisted between us; and by quitting this country for a short time, you . . . might return at leisure, to take possession of your estates for yourself and family." The letter continued with Montague's offer to actually serve under Moultrie if he would agree to espouse the British cause, ending with this now-famous line, "Think well of me."

Moultrie replied, "I am much surprised at your proposition. I flattered myself I stood in a more favorable light with you. But I differ very widely with you, in thinking that I have discharged my duty to my country, while it is still deluged with blood and overrun with British troops, who exercise the most savage cruelties. When I entered into this contest, I did it with the most mature deliberation, and with a determined resolution to risque my life and fortune in the cause. The hardships I have gone through, I look back upon with the greatest pleasure and honor to myself; I shall continue to go on as I have begun, that my example may encourage the youths of America to stand for the defence of their rights and liberties. You call upon me now, and tell me I have a fair opening of quitting that service with honor and reputation to myself, by going with you to Jamaica. Good God! Is it possible that such an idea could arise in the breast of a man of honor? I am sorry you should imagine I have so little regard for my own reputation, as to listen to such dishonorable proposals. Would you wish that a man whom you have honored with your friendship to play the traitor? Surely not." Moultrie's reply ends with the even more famous line, "Think better of me."

Now *that's* the stuff heroes are made of.

Moultrie died in 1805 and was buried at Windsor Hill, just north of Ashley Phosphate Road. Time and vandals have ravaged the cemetery, where for more than a century his grave lay unmarked. Finally in the late 1960s, due to the work of various groups and individuals, the Institute of Archaeology and Anthropology at the University of South Carolina joined in the search for Moultrie's remains. Using modern scientific methods, they found the graves of eight members of Moultrie's family and identified them all. All except the general were re-interred at St. James Goose Creek Church.

On June 28, 1978, Moultrie's remains were re-interred in an elaborate and moving ceremony behind Fort Moultrie, overlooking the Cove. A band in eighteenth century uniforms played the soulful "Dead March" from Handel's oratorio, *Saul*. Then-Governor James B. Edwards delivered an address. Re-enactors from the Second Regiment, South Carolina Line fired a salute at the close of the ceremony. William Moultrie, the great and gallant general, a man of honor and ultimate integrity—a true hero—was home.

Carolina Day

On the morning of the 28th of June I paid a visit to our advance-guard (on horse-back three miles to the eastward of our fort), while I was there, I saw a number of the enemy's boats in motion, at the back of Long-Island, as if they intended a descent upon our advanced post; at the same time, I saw the men-of-war loose their topsails; I hurried back to the fort as fast as possible; when I got there the ships were already under sail; I immediately ordered the long roll to beat, and officers and men to their posts. We had scarcely manned our guns, when the . . . ships of war came sailing up, as if in confidence of victory; as soon as they came within the reach of our guns, we began to fire; they were soon a-breast of the fort . . . let go their anchors . . . and begun their attack most furiously about 10 o'clock, A.M.

—General William Moultrie
from his *Memoirs of the American Revolution*

ONE OF THE THINGS I love best about the islands is trying to imagine what they looked like in earlier years. That three-mile ride Moultrie took on horseback was on a dirt road, which straddled the middle of Sullivan's Island, known today as Middle Street. The advance guard he visited was at Breach Inlet and, surely, as he looked across the inlet to Isle of Palms he had to shield his eyes from the white and brilliant glare of the newly risen sun. Possibly, even with the knowledge that the British were on the move and battle was imminent, some part of him took a moment to appreciate the beauty of that sparkling inlet. Perhaps porpoises were playing in the waters there and the thought passed through his mind that this might be the last time he would ever see those playful creatures. He knew his forces were greatly outnumbered. He had been in battle before and had seen how suddenly death could replace life. As he galloped back to the hastily built palmetto fort at the harbor end of the island, then called Fort Sullivan, he likely considered fate and whether it would work for or against him in the battle that was to come.

He was facing terrible odds. General Sir Henry Clinton had landed upward of 2,500 soldiers on Isle of Palms. Offshore, Admiral Sir Peter Parker's heavily armed war fleet, which included the men-of-war *Bristol, Experiment, Active, Sole-Bay, Syren, Acteon, Sphinx, Friendship* and *Thunder-Bomb*, was maneuvering into readiness. Moultrie, on the other hand, had scarce resources. His armament consisted of a hurriedly found assortment of cannons and only 5,000 pounds of gunpowder. He was undermanned and under-fortified, planning to win a battle from a fort that was still quite unfinished and extremely vulnerable.

Captain Clement Lempriere, described by Moultrie as "a brave and experienced seaman," was with Moultrie when the fleet first came over the bar. Gauging their strength, Lempriere said, "Sir, when those ships come in to lay along side of your fort, they will knock it down in half an hour." Moultrie replied, "then we will lay behind the ruins and prevent their men from landing."

Governor John Rutledge gave Moultrie a single order before the battle began: "Do not make too free with your cannon. Cool and do mischief."

Such an order was perfect for a man with the easy temperament of William Moultrie. Even General Lee, who was often infuriated by Moultrie's insouciant calm, had described him as a man of "good nature and easy temper." When the battle began that morning of June 28, Moultrie calmly held his rein, answering only when necessary and conserving his powder. "Never did men fight more bravely," he wrote afterward, "and never were men more cool (several of the officers, as well as myself, were smoking our pipes and giving orders at the time of the action), their only distress was the want of powder; we had not more than 28 rounds, for 26 guns."

The battle wore on throughout the day, but with remarkably little effect on the palmetto fort. Wrote Moultrie, "They could not make any impression on our fort, built of palmetto logs and filled in with earth, our merlons were 16 feet thick, and high enough to cover the men from the fire of the tops."

When the cannonballs hit the spongy pulp of the palmetto logs, they simply stopped flat, rarely exploding. Others literally sank into the sand. The Americans who were killed or wounded (twelve men killed, twenty-four wounded) received their shots mostly through the embrasures.

Sergeant William Jasper beat all the odds and emerged as a hero. Moultrie wrote, "After some time our flag was shot away . . . and they gave us up all for lost! Supposing that we had struck our flag, and had given up the fort: Sergeant Jasper, perceiving that the flag was shot away . . . jumped from one of the embrasures, and brought it up through a heavy fire, fixed it upon a sponge-staff, and planted it among the ramparts again."

Late that evening, the forces of nature came into play on the side of the Americans with a typical Lowcountry thunderstorm. Moultrie remembered in his memoirs,

Night had closed on the scene . . . [and in] the appearance of a heavy storm, with continual flashes and peals like thunder . . . we came to our slow firing (the ammunition being nearly quite gone) we could hear the shot very distinctly strike the ships: At length the British gave up the conflict: The ships slipt their cables, and dropped down with the tide, and out of reach of our guns.

Early the next morning was presented to our view, the Acteon frigate, hard, and fast aground; at about 400 yards distance; we gave her a few shot, which she returned, but they soon set fire to her, and quitted her; Capt. Jacob Milligan and others, went in some of our boats, boarded her while she was on fire, and pointed 2 or 3 guns at the Commodore, and fired them; then brought off the ships bell, and other articles, and had scarcely left her, when she blew up, and from the explosion issued a grand pillar of smoke, which soon expanded itself at the top, and to appearance, formed the figure of a palmetto tree.

The battle was won. It was the first significant victory for the Americans against the British. The stories of Fort Sullivan became a rallying cry for other patriots and, less than a week later, the Declaration of Independence was signed in Philadelphia. The United States of America was born.

Carolina Day has been celebrated every year since 1777. As you fly your South Carolina state flag and gaze at the silhouette of a palmetto tree on the flag's brilliant field of blue, remember that the freedoms we now take for granted were hard fought by men who, like William Moultrie, with nothing more than sand, palmetto logs and sheer determination, made a stand that helped change the course of American history.

Crossing the Breach

T HE BEAUTIFUL INLET SEPARATING ISLE of Palms and Sullivan's Island
is not only known for its history (and good fishing)—it has a long-
standing reputation for unpredictability. One moment, the water's surface is calm and smooth as glass. The tide changes, the wind comes up,
and faster than you can say, "Look! A porpoise!" the water is a boiling
mass of currents, eddies, and whirlpools.

It is deceptively shallow in places and, in others, deceptively deep—
as much as thirty feet. An immense amount of water pours through this
narrow passage with each tidal change and, like a huge maritime drill,
scours out holes and dredges the depths. You can be safely standing on
hard-packed sand at the water's edge when, suddenly, the sand gives
way and you're sucked into water well over your head. It is *not* a place
for swimming. Large signs are posted warning people to stay out of the
water. Still, each year some foolhardy soul decides he knows better and
gets in trouble, or worse. Tragically, drownings occur every year.

I have always felt that if we were to place signs on each side of
Breach Inlet which read "DANGEROUS: SHARK-INFESTED WA-
TERS!" people might pay attention. The inlet's rushing tide carries a
tremendous amount of marine life and other nutrients that make up
the oceanic food chain. Consequently, it is where fish feed. And where

fish feed, sharks feed. I saw the largest shark I have ever seen in my life at Breach Inlet. I am told it was a Tiger Shark, known as a "man-eater," a frightening leviathan that was some twelve feet long. It swam blithely by me as I stood on the shore, fishing, so close I felt I could reach out and touch it. Not that I wanted to—but it was an experience that gave me an entirely new respect for the creatures lurking beneath the surface of Breach Inlet's waters.

The inlet's historical beginning is not exactly known. It seems logical that it may have received its name when, at some point in history, a breach occurred which separated the islands. Inlets are often formed or changed this way, especially during severe hurricanes. There were several such storms between the first settlement in 1670 and 1700, when the inlet was called by name by explorer John Lawson. On his journey northward, while attempting to cross "the Breach," he noted in his diary that "we had not Water enough for our Craft to go over, although we drew but two Foot, or thereabouts." They eventually crossed at full tide.

Seventy-six years later, the inlet foiled another attempted crossing, but this time it wasn't the inlet's shallowness, but its exceptional depth that proved frustrating. In June 1776, British General Sir Henry Clinton, commanding approximately 2,500 British soldiers encamped on Isle of Palms, was gearing up for an attack on the newly-erected fortification at the harbor's mouth, Fort Sullivan. His plan was to invade Sullivan's Island from the north while the British fleet attacked from seaward. Clinton had been assured that the inlet was shallow enough to ford on foot.

"To our unspeakable mortification," Clinton wrote later, "a channel which for some time before was reported to have been only eighteen inches deep at low water, was now found to be seven feet—a circumstance, I am told, not uncommon to this coast."

Furthermore, the Americans had well-positioned batteries of sharpshooters on the Sullivan's Island side of the inlet who, under the direction of Colonel William Thomson (at times spelled as "Thompson") were laying in wait. When the British attempted to cross on the morning of June 28, 1776, they were met with a well-aimed barrage. "Our rifles were in prime order, well proved and well charged," wrote North Carolinian Morgan Brown, one of the American sharpshooters, of the raking the British took that day. "Every man took deliberate aim at his object . . . The fire taught the enemy to lie closer behind their bank of oysters, and only show themselves when they rose up to fire." Clinton's inability to "cross the breach" played a significant part in the American's ultimate victory over the British. The failed assault on Fort Sullivan was a major defeat, one they did not suffer gladly. The British did not attempt to attack Charleston again for four years.

Breach Inlet also played a considerable role during the Civil War. The Confederates erected a battery on the Sullivan's Island side near the same spot where Thomson's Revolutionary War battery had been placed a century before. Built in 1863 and named to honor Confederate General J. Foster Marshall, Battery Marshall carried an armament of fourteen various-caliber smoothbores, rifles and howitzers.

Also, it was in the inlet's depths that the submarine USS *Hunley* practiced training dives, and it was from Breach Inlet that the *Hunley* left on the night of February 17, 1864, to engage the Federal corvette USS *Housatonic.* Upon impact, the *Housatonic* sank almost immediately. The *Hunley* was lost, as well, with all men aboard. It was the first successful attack of a submarine on a surface ship in naval history.

During World War II, a new Fort Marshall was erected overlooking Breach Inlet and the remains of this fortification, large hills that enclosed gun emplacements, are today private homes. Officially called "Construction 520," Fort Marshall had an armament of two 12-inch Model 1895-MI guns, set 420 feet apart and sited to allow each of the two guns a field of fire of 145 degrees. Although they were never used in combat, they had the capacity of firing a 975-pound projectile 29,300 yards, with each gun capable of firing one-and-a-half rounds per minute.

It wasn't until 1898 that there was a bridge across Breach Inlet, built to carry passengers to the new Isle of Palms resort on the trolley line. Describing this bridge as a "fine piece of work," the *News & Courier* reported that it "stands as solidly as a brick wall against the ebb and flow of the tide." Including its approaches it was 1,200 feet long. "This bridge over Breach Inlet is considered quite an engineering feat, as many people thought it was not possible to bridge the inlet," wrote the *Courier.* "But it has been done and successfully done, for though the tide was rushing through the inlet at a tremendous pace, those who were in the car felt as though they were riding on solid ground, and were only reminded of the fact that they were in reality crossing the water by looking out upon the rippling waves on either side of the car."

Today, the only "warfare" that occurs around inlet waters is now of the natural type—skimmers versus minnows, pelicans diving for fish and crab against crabber. Its approaches change with every tide and a sandbar you walked on yesterday may not be there tomorrow, replaced instead by a new, narrow channel where the outgoing tide sweeps by with enough energy to run a host of generators.

Breach Inlet is a beautiful, integral part of the barrier island eco-system. It funnels food from the marshes, which give sustenance to the creatures of the sea. Its perpetual movement is its constancy—the epitome of the ever-changing continuum called the Carolina coast.

Early Sullivan's Island Laws

Whereas, the inhabitants of Sullivan's Island have petitioned the Legislature to grant an act for incorporation . . . from the unusual prevalence and alarming effects of the yellow fever during the past summer and autumn in Charleston, not only to strangers, but to native inhabitants, particularly of the younger class, that Island hath been, and probably hereafter must be greatly resorted to as an asylum.

—*From an Act to Incorporate Moultrieville*
passed December 17, 1817

THERE ARE UNDOUBTEDLY THOSE WHO *still* maintain that Sullivan's Island is an "asylum," and, having spent a good number of my growing-up years on the island, I'm not the one to argue with them. I remember when they bricked and boarded up the forts in the 1960s after the Cuban Missile Crisis to make bomb shelters. My mother watched the progress from our house near the fort and said, with kind sarcasm, "Oh, good . . . we'll have nuclear war and the only people who'll live through it to procreate the new world will be the year-round residents of Sullivan's Island!" Frankly, knowing the people on the island back then, how nice they were and what a true sense of community there was, Mother's prophecy wouldn't have been such a bad idea.

But I digress. This is about times on the island much earlier, when the island population, at least in the summertime, often surpassed the number of people on the island today.

Up until the late 1700s, not much was happening on the island, at least not from a civilian standpoint. But from 1790 to 1817, after year upon year of deadly diseases attacking the people of Charleston, with yellow fever and smallpox leading the list, it was soon discovered that the "salubrious" air of Sullivan's Island not only helped prevent, but also often helped cure sicknesses. People started coming to the island each summer in droves—they called it "resorting to" the island—and by the early 1800s a sizable summer community had grown up on the south end of the island. Finally, in 1817, these summer residents decided to incorporate as a township under the name of "Moultrieville," with all the laws and legalities such incorporation required.

One of the first acts was to name commissioners to lay out streets. Those gentlemen were Colonel Lewis Morris, William Henry DeSaussure, Frederick Rutledge, Jacob Sass and William Robertson. This act, predictably, was followed by an act to assess (tax) the inhabitants to offset the cost of surveying and laying out the streets.

Once they got the business of people and taxes straight, what do you suppose was the next law they passed? It was a law to prohibit gambling on Sunday: "That if any person shall keep or suffer to be kept, any gaming table, or permit any game or games to be played in his, her or their houses . . . on the Sabbath day . . . shall be fined the sum of fifty dollars."

Of course, once they'd gotten it straight that there would be no gambling on Sunday, they then followed with a law to *license* billiard and gaming places (for a fee, of course) as well as those people keeping taverns and retailing spirituous liquors.

One of my favorites is the speed limit law: "It shall not be lawful for any person driving a cart, dray, chair, carriage, or any other vehicle, on the beach of the Island . . . any faster than a walk, trot, or pace, and by no means to gallop any horse or horses, that are drawing any carriage or vehicle, under a penalty of five dollars." Likewise, it was illegal to shoot game on the beach. The curlew grounds were a favorite place to shoot birds and at that time people ate almost every bird that flew, with the possible exception of the seagull. The law stated that "it shall not be lawful, for any person or persons, to take a station or stand on the front beach, or within one hundred and fifty yards of high water mark, or any part of the front of the Island, for the purpose of shooting at game." The penalty was five dollars for each and every offense, which leads one to believe that this was a law rather frequently ignored.

Thinking of going skinny-dipping? This was apparently a frequent enough practice in the early 1800s to require this law: "That it shall not be lawful for any adult person, to bathe openly and naked in the waters contiguous to the beach, at any time of the day after the rising of the sun, or until two hours after sunset." It was okay to swim unclothed at night. Just watch out for sharks.

Here's one that I bet a lot of folks would like to see made into law again: It was actually against the law to work on Sunday, and "if any tradesmen, artificer, workman, laborer, or any other person, shall do . . . any worldly labour, business or work of their ordinary callings upon Sunday, on Sullivan's Island (works of necessity or charity only excepted) . . . such personal shall forfeit and pay for every such offence a fine not exceeding five dollars."

Under the heading of "some things never change," there was a law preventing the cutting of trees. "It shall not be lawful for any person or persons, at any time to cut down and make use of the Cedars, or other trees on the east end of this Island, known as the Myrtles, for posts, ship timber, or for any other purpose whatsoever, except for fascines to resist the encroachment of the sea." Lawmakers well recognized the buffer against the ocean these wild places provided. This law, I believe, is still on the books.

Animals have always been a problem—both alive and dead. One law stated that "if any horse, cow, dog, or any other animal, the property of any person whomsoever, shall die in any part of Sullivan's Island, it shall be the duty of the owner . . . to bury the carcass at least three feet under the ground . . . or on the shore of the waters of the Cove, far remote from the landing." It was also okay to take the carcass to the front beach and let it float off with the outgoing tide, just as long as it didn't float back ashore with the next tide.

As far as live animals were concerned, no swine or goats were allowed to run at large, and if found out of their owner's enclosures, they could be "destroyed or seized by any person or persons, and converted to his or her . . . own use."

And finally, there were dogs. An act of 1844 refers to dogs running at large as "an evil of such magnitude," that it required a special ordinance. Of course, this was at a time prior to the discovery of a cure for rabies and if bitten by a rabid dog, a person would (and they did) die. Still, dogs were a major part of people's daily lives (as they still are today) and there was some leniency. The act read "no dog shall be allowed to go at large in any street, lane or common on said Island, from the first day of May to the first of November in each and every year." People who were "accompanied by dogs in the streets or in public" were required to have their dog "muzzled, or secured by a sufficient rope, cord or chain." If a dog was found running at large, the ordinance authorized people "to kill any dog or dogs going at large . . . and . . . producing proof of his having killed any dog, pursuant to this Ordinance . . . shall receive a reward of fifty cents." Apparently this law did not require dogs to be leashed on the beach and one writer of the period, Caroline Gilman, wrote of an island beach scene as familiar today as it was to her in the 1840s: "How happy were they all . . . Generous boys and gentle girls in innocent joy . . . gathered rough shells, and threw them in the dark waters, greeted their conscious dog as he came dripping, with some prize from the surge; wrote sweet names on the beach, ran and shouted in careless laughter against the breeze, or mused on those thoughts which come even to childhood from the bounding sea." That's the best thing about the island: Some things never change.

Osceola on Sullivan's Island

Hᴉ*s* ɢʀᴀᴠᴇ ɪs ᴊᴜsᴛ ᴛᴏ the right of the main entrance to Fort Moultrie. The flat stone marker reads "OCEOLA. Patriot and Warrior. Died at Fort Moultrie. January 30th, 1838."

Who was this man, this mighty Seminole warrior who had been a
feared and open enemy of the American soldier, and how did he come
to be given a hero's burial at the entrance of a fortification belonging
to his greatest enemy?

His is a story with heroics worthy of a movie script. Osceola was
born around 1804 in present-day Macon County, Alabama. He was
an Upper Creek Indian, a Muskogee, and his name is thought to
be an Anglicized version of the word Asi, meaning "Black Drink"
and Yaholo, or "Singer." In his youth, Osceola was also known by
another name, Billy Powell, for his Muskogee mother had married
a white trader named William Powell. Osceola later renounced this
name and is said to have declared emphatically, "No foreign blood
runs in my veins, I am pure-blood Muskogee." From the Indian
point of view, he was correct. Their tribal structure was matrilineal,
with descent and inheritance coming from the mother's side. Also,
as his father left early in Osceola's life, he was raised entirely as a
Muskogee.

By 1830, when President Andrew Jackson's Indian Removal Bill was put into effect, Osceola was fully affiliated with the Florida Seminole, an amalgamated "tribe" created from the remnants of displaced Indians from throughout the south. He was married (twice, as was the Seminole custom for men) and was becoming more and more respected for his physical strength and leadership. Also living with the Seminole were a large number of runaway slaves and free blacks, many who had been with the Seminole for two or three generations; some historians believe Osceola's second wife may have been black. The wild swamp lands of Florida were one of the few remaining places left to the southeastern Indians, and it was for the right to retain this homeland that the strong and handsome young warrior fought so bravely.

Osceola was about thirty-one when, on April 23, 1835, Indian agent Wiley Thompson met with Seminole leaders in hopes of getting them to sign a new treaty. Not only did the new treaty break a previous one, which guaranteed the Seminole their lands in Florida, it included their forced removal to lands west. It also meant that slave catchers and traders could take the blacks among them (both freemen and fugitive slaves) into bondage. After making a long, pontifical speech, Thompson asked for signatures. The top chief, Micanopy, had already refused. A few chiefs nodded but four refused: Alligator, Arpeika, Black Dirt and Jumper. When it came time for Osceola to put his signature on the treaty, it is said that he drew his hunting knife and stabbed it down savagely at the table, crying, "This is the only way I sign!" When Thompson reported the treaty refusal back to Jackson, he responded by ordering a "sufficient military force" to Florida to physically remove the tribe. This was the beginning of what would be known as the Second Seminole War.

Osceola was a natural choice as the war leader for the Seminole. Prior to hostilities, he had worked closely with the white soldiers at various Florida forts as a runner and guide. He had formed close friendships and become extremely knowledgeable of the white man's military ways. This, along with his own natural tactical brilliance, soon paid off. Not only did he teach his own warriors how to fight as a working unit, he artfully manipulated the Seminole's familiarity of the swamps to the detriment of the white soldiers, who were soon bogged down in the deep morasses, handicapped by the army's stolid, European-style tactics. For two years, the Seminole crushed the military, and battle after bloody battle resulted in Seminole victory.

Interestingly, the American public had mixed feelings about what was happening to the Seminole. Many were appalled at the government's position and even men actually involved in the fight were horrified at the numerous broken treaties and blatant lies committed by various officials. One letter to the *Charleston Courier*, written on December 29, 1837, signed by "An Officer of the 4th Artillery, Camp St. Johns," noted, "they are now clinging with the last efforts of despair to their beloved homes. Can any Christian in the Republic know this and still pray for the continuance of blessing when he is about to wrest from the unhappy Seminoles all that the Great Spirit ever conferred upon him?"

It was pure treachery that eventually led to Osceola's capture. Tired of war and tired of fighting, the Seminole were ready to meet with U.S. representatives to search for a way to end the hostilities and still keep their lands. The American government, represented by General Thomas S. Jesup, agreed to meet the Seminole. When Osceola and his warriors arrived under a white flag of truce, Jesup ordered the Indians surrounded and taken prisoner. Jesup's action horrified the nation. Even so, Osceola, several chiefs (including Micanophy and King Philip), 116 warriors and 82 women and children (including Osceola's own family), were put aboard the S.S. *Poinsett* and shipped to Fort Moultrie, arriving on January 1, 1838.

In 1898, historian Charles H. Coe wrote of Osceola: "The fearless bravery and manly qualities of this chief, his unusual knowledge of scientific warfare and, above all, his unswerving determination to defend to the last his chosen home, had spread his fame throughout the length and breadth of the country, and won for him respect and admiration, even in the hearts of his bitterest enemies." Osceola was an instant celebrity. On January 6, he and the other chiefs were taken to the Charleston Theater to see a play called *Honey-Moon*. On January 17, the artist George Catlin arrived at Fort Moultrie to paint the Seminole chieftains, and his painting of Osceola is one of his most famous.

Having long suffered from a malarial illness, on the night of January 26, 1838, Osceola was stricken with quinsy, a severe and painful swelling of the throat accompanied by high fever. According to the doctor

who attended him, Dr. Frederick Weedon, Osceola, knowing that he
was about to die,

*made signs for his wives to go and bring his full dress which he wore in time of war
. . . rose up in his bed, which was on the floor and put on his shirt, his leggings and
his moccasins, girded on his war belt, bullet-pouch and powder horn, and laid his
knife by the side of him on the floor. He then . . . painted one half of his face his
neck and his throat with vermilion, a custom practiced when the irrevocable oath of
war and destruction is taken. His knife he then placed in its sheath under his belt,
and he carefully arranged his turban on his head and his three ostrich plumes that he
was in the habit of wearing in it.*

*Being thus prepared in full dress, he lay down a few moments to recover strength
sufficiently, when he rose up as before, and with most benignant and pleasing smiles,
extended his hand to me and to all the officers and chiefs that were around him, and
shook hands with us all in dead silence, and with his wives and little children.*

*He made a signal for them to lower him down upon his bed, which was done, and
he then slowly drew from his war-belt his scalping-knife, which he firmly grasped in
his right hand, laying it across the other on his breast, and in a moment smiled away
his last breath without a struggle or groan.*

He was buried with full military honors the following day at the gate
of the fort. Despite his imprisonment, Osceola was never conquered.
He never surrendered the Seminole as a nation and the American government was never successful in moving all the Seminole westward. As
the historian Coe wrote, "His fame will never die; centuries will come
and go, but the name of Osceola will remain as long as the earth is
peopled."

Two if by Sea:
Our Charleston Lighthouses

FROM THE SEA, THE FIRST two things you see even before you spot land are Charleston's two lighthouses—the modern, sharp-edged, black-and-white Sullivan's Island light on the right and, on the left, the elegant, traditional curves of the old Morris Island light. Like fraternal twins born a century apart, both have shared the name "Charleston Light." The two being similar, yet each retaining a unique individuality, they frame the entrance to Charleston harbor. And, like the city they protect, they are a melding of old and new, of past meeting present, architectural masterpieces tenaciously upholding a time-honored duty.

Today, the Morris Island light is entirely surrounded by water, the sea having claimed the land on which it originally stood. Its lenses are extinguished and it now functions only as a day mark. Built between 1876 and 1885, this sturdy, 158-foot brick edifice saw almost a century of active duty until 1962, when old gave way to new with the erection of the Sullivan's Island light. Historically, this wasn't the first time the Charleston Light had switched from one island to the other. Ironically, each change came about because the lights stood precariously on shifting sands.

The very first lighthouse to mark Charleston's harbor was built on Sullivan's Island in the 1670s, a sparse wooden tower lit with "fier balls of pitch and ocum." Oakum, a material made from hemp, provided the light's wick, which was burned with tar, or pitch, in an iron basket on top of the tower. The tower served a dual purpose, not only providing a beacon for approaching ships, but also acting as a watchtower from which lookouts searched for approaching vessels.

In 1702, an act to make Sullivan's Island "More Remarkable to Mariners" was passed to replace the wooden lookout, which had been "overthrown to the ground" after the severe hurricane of 1700. The new beacon was to be made of brick, described as being "Twenty five foot Diamitir at Bottome and Twelve feete, Diamiter at Topp, with Two flores and that the foundation to be . . . secured with Pyles." It was also this act that resulted in what would now be seen as rash: the clear-cutting of Sullivan's Island. The act required that "all the underwoods . . . and such other of the standing and growing trees . . . be cut down and cleared . . . and [only] the remarkable trees left standing in such form and figure as they most conduce to the better distinguishing of said Island." In the absence of a standing beacon, ships could find the entrance to Charleston by simply looking for the island *without* any trees.

In 1713, another hurricane destroyed the Sullivan's Island beacon. An act was passed for the erection of a bigger and better tower, which was to be raised under the direction of fearless pirate fighter Colonel William Rhett and was to be "no less in height than sixty feet." By this time, burning tallow candles provided the necessary light. Later, fish oil was burned in lamps suspended from the dome of the tower.

Still, even solid brick could not halt the encroaching sea. In 1752, the Sullivan's Island light was destroyed by yet another hurricane. With a history of so many lighthouses on that island either "overthrown" or "washed" by storms, it was decided to move the main Charleston Light across the harbor to the more stable Morris Island, then called "Middle Island" or "Middle Bay Island." A notice in the *Gazette* on December 1, 1766, read: "A beacon is forthwith to be erected upon Middle Bay Island, near the bar, to be built of brick, 115 feet high, with a lanthorn on the top. Mr. Samuel Cardy, we hear, has been contracted with . . . the building thereof."

Interestingly, Cardy had also been the builder of St. Michael's Church on the corner of Meeting and Broad Streets, completed in 1762. The church's graceful, white steeple was noted, even before its completion, as a "lighthouse" in its own right. In 1755, with building funds exhausted and the spire only two-thirds complete, the church appealed to the South Carolina Assembly for help, writing "that the Steeple . . . as besides being an Ornament to Charlestown . . . it is of extraordinary Use to the Navigation on our Coast. It is so high as to be discerned at Sea before the Land is Seen & is so properly situated as to be a plain leading mark for the Bar of this Harbour, and therefore effectually answers the Purpose and Intention of building a Beacon, which expence may be thereby saved to this Province." In answer, money originally earmarked for building a new lighthouse went to the completion of St. Michael's steeple.

By 1765, the need for a permanent lighthouse at the harbor entrance was evident and Cardy's lighthouse was finished in 1767. This first "Morris Island Light," 115 feet high and octagonal, was one of the first eight of such "permanent" lighthouses built in America. Its importance to Charleston's growing shipping industry is evidenced by visitor Josiah Quincy, who wrote in 1773 that there were "a smaller number" of vessels in Charleston than usual, only "about 350 sail." This lighthouse remained until 1857 when a new beacon was built on Morris Island, standing 133 feet high and illuminated with that new, modern invention, the Fresnel lens. This lighthouse had a short life. In 1861, with the Federal blockading fleet offshore, the Confederate government ordered all harbor lights extinguished and the lighthouse was destroyed.

The present Morris Island light was begun in 1876. Constructed of brick and 33 feet in diameter at the base, it stands 158 feet above sea level and is topped by a lantern and parapet gallery made of iron. Built under the same guidelines as North Carolina's Cape Hatteras, Bodie Island and Cape Lookout lighthouses, its markings—black-and-white horizontal bands—were designed to be easily discernible and stand out against the sky. It has withstood repeated hurricanes. What hasn't survived is the land on which it was built.

Changing currents resulting from the building of the jetties have drastically changed the face of Morris Island. The island is now less than one-third of its original size and what is left is actually the narrow, back strip of the island. Gone are the lighthouse keeper's cottage, the outbuildings and the tall dunes. Now the lighthouse stands, alone, far from the beach and in the sea.

Two hundred years after it had been moved to Morris Island, the Charleston Light once more returned to Sullivan's Island. On June 15, 1962, the Sullivan's Island lighthouse went into operation. It has three rotating lenses with a potential power of 28 million candles and stands 165 feet high. First manned by the U.S. Coast Guard, it became fully automated in 1982. Originally painted red and white, it was built three-sided to withstand hurricane-force winds. It stood its first test with Hurricane Hugo. Time and the tides will only tell whether it will continue to withstand the natural forces of an encroaching sea.

Most important, it stands the test of daily use. The Sullivan's Island light stands as a landmark to all manner of sea-going vessels, from the smallest pleasure boat to skyscraper-tall, football fields-long container ships. On a marine chart, it is marked simply as "Charleston Light." Yet, like its many historical predecessors, this tall, illuminated structure is more than a simple light. It is the mariner's guidepost, a welcoming beacon lighting the path to the harbor, leading the way to safe anchorage.

The Lighthouse
and Colonel Ulmo

In 1960 I was twelve years old and my family lived on Sullivan's Island near Station 19, on I'on Avenue just a short block from the Coast Guard Station. Ours was a typical island summer house of the nineteenth century—a rambling, high-ceilinged, porch-surrounded affair with more rooms than purpose (it could sleep eighteen), hidden by a tangle of trees on a half-acre lot next to Battery Gadsden. My bedroom on the southwest side adjoined a screened-in sleeping porch with a grouping of iron beds in various stages of island-humidity rust. The pillows were hard as rocks; the sheets rough from years of starch and always riddled with sand. In the summer dampness, the sheets stuck to my legs.

I didn't care. The sleeping porch was cool on hot summer nights and as close as one could get to sleeping outside, without mosquitoes. The house was set up high on stilts and almost entirely surrounded by trees, thus the sleeping porch was practically in the boughs. I would usually awake long before sunrise with the first chirpings of the birds. Listening to their soft twitters and chirrups I'd roll over and dreamily fall back into a second slumber until it was time to get up.

The "alarm" that awoke me the second time was the sound of the ship's bells from the Coast Guard Station marking the hour. Back then, the Coast Guard Station was still active, a busy installation run with relaxed spit-and-polish by John Midgett, a Hatteras-born colossus who belied his name by standing six feet, four inches in size fifteen shoes.

One didn't need a watch to know the time on Sullivan's Island in those days. The Coast Guard bells rang the watch every half-hour with Greenwich-time preciseness. Noon arrived, compliments of the Volunteer Fire Department and the wail of their siren. It started low and slow, eventually ascending into a mournful, high-pitched "AH-WOOOO-OO-OO" that brought every dog on the island into a frenzy of yowls as they tried (with fine success) to match its piercing tones.

It was in these years that another sound also filled the island air—the deep, reverberating, KA-THOOMPA, KA-THOOMPA of the pile driver boring footings deep into the island's subsoil on the grassy lawn in front of the Coast Guard Station. A mammoth structure was under construction—the Sullivan's Island lighthouse.

Back then, when the island's year-round population was only around 200 people, even small news was big news. The construction of the lighthouse was BIG news. It took two years to build and thus provided fodder for two years of armchair critique.

"It's going to sink. Ain't nothing holding this island up but water," the naysayers entoned. "Just you watch; come next hurricane the whole damned thing'll blow down."

Leading this fray was the self-appointed "commandant" of Sullivan's Island, Colonel Harry Ulmo. A short, compact man of ceaseless military correctness, Ulmo had been assigned to Fort Moultrie before the war. After the fort's deactivation and his retirement, he and his wife Dorothy decided to make the island their permanent home.

Colonel Ulmo was a man accustomed to giving orders and having them followed. The fact that Fort Moultrie was no longer active and his rank was now that of civilian made not one iota of difference to Colonel Ulmo. He continued to dress in military khakis. His tie was always neatly tucked into his shirt between the first and second button. His head was never without his Army-issued kepi. He made everyone's business his own (whether they liked it or not), and ran the island with bulldog persistence. Not surprisingly, the building of the lighthouse became Ulmo's particular pet project.

To the workmen involved with its construction, the men who had to suffer the unsolicited advice he shouted over the din of the pile drivers, Colonel Ulmo was undoubtedly their own pet peeve.

Since Colonel and Mrs. Ulmo lived in the house next to ours, we saw more of "the Colonel" than most. I can still see him in my mind's eye, sitting at parade rest in our back yard in a straight-backed wooden chair, berating the flock of seagulls that flew in daily to steal the bird food out of my mother's feeders.

"Shoo!" he'd bark. "That's an order, now! SHOO! SKEDADDLE!" The gulls, of course, ignored his blustering, as did we. He was a colonel without a post; a man who had spent his entire life getting the job done. And now, there was no job to do.

So the Colonel spent his days hassling the seagulls, straightening out the way mail was handled by Miss Katy at the post office, arguing over the price of porkchops at the island's grocery store, Ogletree's, and complaining to Dr. Bert Wurthmann about the "drugstore cowboys" hanging around the soda fountain at his pharmacy. And God help the poor soul who had the misfortune of crossing the causeway behind the Colonel when he decided to drive to Mount Pleasant. He took the road at a steady twenty-five miles per hour, both hands firmly on the wheel, cursing those who dared pass him as speed-demons and dang-blasted fools.

Thus it is not surprising that, for the two years the lighthouse was under construction, the Colonel took to "supervising" its progress with characteristic vigor. The workmen were good sports. They would listen patiently as he barked instructions—told them what they were doing wrong, how to fix it and what they should do next. They suffered his officiousness with grace and the occasional salute, knowing he would eventually toddle off to mind someone else's business and they could get back to theirs.

Despite the Colonel's unbidden directives, the construction of the lighthouse continued. We islanders watched in wonder as the steel framework took shape and this strange, triangular structure began to soar upward. Before we knew it, it was finished. The powerful lights were positioned with not just one, but *three* lenses designed to rotate in a sequence that would be recognized by ships offshore. The island was bursting with pride. Not only did our lighthouse have three lights, it was purportedly the most powerful lighthouse in the western hemisphere! Finally, the long-awaited evening came when they were turned on for the first time.

If you look at the lighthouse today you will see that the rear portion of the lights window is shielded. Only narrow slits open onto the landward side. Yet on the night the lighthouse was first illuminated—with its brightest, most intense power—the back of the lights window was as exposed as the front. That night (and every night for the next several weeks) the entire island was saturated with light every time the lenses made their rotation. Light flooded into homes and yards, intermittently turning darkness into day, entering bedrooms and front piazzas with every rotation of the powerful beams.

It was maddening. There would be complete darkness, then . . . LIGHT! Then darkness again, a pause, and . . . LIGHT! Dark, pause . . . LIGHT! All night long. Sleep deprivation was aggravated by the fact that this also caused the island dogs to dissemble into convulsions of barking, including the Colonel's two ancient pointers, Spot and Fanny, who could howl with the gusto of wolves on a full moon. The Colonel was about to split a gusset.

"Dadburn fools!" he sputtered. "I TOLD them that light was too strong!" The Colonel was also the ringleader of islanders who firmly believed that lights with such intensity were bad for a person's health. Just like those "damned sputniks" orbiting the earth in space were, in the Colonel's estimation, causing everything from severe tropical weather to flu epidemics.

"Dangerous, that's what they are!" he bellowed. "If a man was to stand right next to one of those lights, he'd get burned alive!" The Colonel was ready to climb the lighthouse steps and personally pull the plug.

He didn't need to. The windows were eventually shielded and the power dimmed to a lesser intensity. Nor did the lighthouse fall down with the next hurricane, or sink into the island's soft sand. It instead became the island's cherished darling, as synonymous with Sullivan's Island as the beach at low tide.

Today, the Coast Guard Station is no longer active and the light is fully automated. Yet the lighthouse stands, ever watchful, a welcoming beacon to ships far out at sea, a testimony to superb engineering and a team of workmen who, from driving the pilings to the installation of the lenses, did their job with remarkable skill—and despite the aggravation of dealing with Colonel Ulmo.

Ah, but I know something and, now, so do you. Only one person is *really* responsible for building that lighthouse, for making certain its construction was accomplished with requisite military exactitude—Colonel Harry Ulmo. He died many years ago but, if the lighthouse could speak, I'm sure it would say, "Yes, SIR! Colonel Ulmo. The lights are ON, Colonel Ulmo! And sir? You did a damned fine job!"

Poe on Sullivan's Island

ONE OF THE MORE FAMOUS people to spend time on Sullivan's Island was Edgar Allan Poe. It was in November 1827 that Poe came to Sullivan's Island under his own shroud of mystery. Arriving on the brig *Waltham* with other recruits bound for Fort Moultrie, Poe had enlisted under the alias "Edgar A. Perry." Name was not the only thing Poe had falsified, he also claimed his age as twenty-two, when he was actually only eighteen. Using an assumed name was not new to Po. Just prior to his enlistment he had been living in Boston under the name of "Henri Le Rennet."

Why the aliases? In 1826, Poe was forced to leave his studies at the University of Virginia after incurring tremendous gambling debts. His infuriated stepfather refused to pay the debts and the two became estranged. Poe then moved to Boston and began writing. In short order, his financial state bordered on destitution. It can only be presumed that Poe chose to remove himself as far as possible from his family, his finances and his despair over both. What is certain is that while on Sullivan's Island, Poe grew to admire coastal life, its history, flora and fauna, eventually using it as the setting for his famous tale of buried pirate's treasure, *The Gold Bug*, which he wrote in 1843. He begins this short story by describing the island in less than flattering prose:

The island is a very singular one. It consists of little else than sea sand, and is about three miles long. Its breadth at no point exceeds a quarter of a mile. It is separated from the main land by a scarcely perceptible creek, oozing its way through a wilderness of reeds and slime, a favorite resort for the marsh hen. The vegetation, as might be supposed, is scant, or least dwarfish. No trees of any magnitude are to be seen. Near the western extremity, where Fort Moultrie stands, and where are some miserable frame buildings, tenanted during summer, by the fugitives from Charleston dust and fever, may be found, indeed the bristly palmetto; but the whole island, with the exception of this western point, and a line of hard, white beach on the seacoast, is covered with a dense undergrowth of the sweet myrtle.

Today, the "miserable frame buildings" have been replaced by substantial homes. Fort Moultrie still stands guard, not as a military base but as a National Park monument. The mainland of Mount Pleasant is, depending on bridge openings, easily accessible by a causeway cutting through the "reed and marshes" which still remain a favorite place for the marsh hen.

The Gold Bug. Did such a creature exist? Is there a possibility that pirate treasure lays hidden somewhere along the East Cooper coastline? Is there any truth to Poe's fiction, or was it simply a good story?

In the 1820s, Fort Moultrie was an outpost on an island inhabited almost exclusively by summer "resorters." Poe's position as company clerk apparently gave the young poet a considerable amount of free time to ponder, although at his young age, one doubts that his pondering was "weak and weary." In all likelihood, much of his free time was spent walking on the beach. Having a natural proclivity toward science and nature, it is entirely likely that Poe befriended Dr. Edmund Ravenel. Ravenel summered on the island and at times served as Fort Moultrie's physician and as the island's intendant, or mayor. Ravenel was on his way to becoming internationally famous as a conchologist and spent much of his time studying the island's natural habitat, especially marine shells. He eventually catalogued over 3,500 specimens and the South Carolina state shell, the lettered olive, has the Latin name *Olividae ravenelsis.*

Many literary historians believe that Poe's character of Legrand in *The Gold Bug* was based on Dr. Ravenel. Certainly, with Ravenel's close involvement both with natural history and the island, the theory is plausible. "In the inmost recesses of this coppice, not far from the eastern or more remote end of the island, Legrand had built himself a small hut. . . . He had with him many books, but rarely employed them. His chief amusements were gunning and fishing, or sauntering along the beach and through the myrtles, in quest of shells or entomological specimens;—his collection of the latter might have been envied by a Swammerdam." (Jan Swammerdam was a Dutch naturalist of the 1600s.)

Poe's story continues with Legrand discovering a most unusual beetle of "a brilliant gold color—about the size of a large hickory nut—with two jet black spots near one extremity of the back," which gave the hideous impression of a skull, or death's head. This discovery leads Legrand to an ancient parchment on which a map is drawn, in secret code, bearing the mark of a goat, or kid.

How much of this story is true? There is a type of "gold" bug native to the islands called *Callichroma splendidum,* a rather large beetle, or *scarabaeus,* marked with greenish and gold hues. There is no death's head marking on this beetle but then, Poe was a master at using his imagination to take something like a harmless bug and turn it, fictionally, into something macabre.

Legrand found the pirate's map "about a mile east-ward of the island, and but a short distance above high water mark." Legrand describes finding "a scrap of parchment, which I then supposed to be paper . . . lying half buried in the sand, a corner sticking up. Near the spot where we found it, I observed the remnants of the hull of what appeared to have been a ship's long boat."

Aha! There is only one place situated a mile eastward of Sullivan's Island, and that is Isle of Palms. In Poe's time the island was remote and totally uninhabited. As for finding the ancient hull of a pirate's long boat? A hundred years earlier, pirates had been the scourges of the Carolina coast.

Here Poe's historical accuracy ends. The encoded map Legrand finds is marked with a picture of a goat, or kid—alluding to the famous pirate Captain Kidd. Lowcountry waters saw a number of ferocious pirates, including the most dreaded pirate of all, Blackbeard. Captain Kidd's territory was up east, from New York to Nova Scotia, not South Carolina.

After decoding the map, Legrand, his Negro slave Jupiter and the unnamed narrator of the story then journey to the main land to search for the treasure. They "cross the creek at the head of the island by means of a skiff, and ascending the high grounds on the shore of the main land, proceeded in a northwesterly direction, through a country excessively wild and desolate, where no trace of a human footstep was to be seen."

The creek they took could either be Conch Creek or Inlet Creek, both of which still weave their way toward mainland Mount Pleasant. In the 1820s, however, this mainland was fairly well settled plantation land. Poe's reality of the area is completely fictitious when he begins describing the topography. They came ashore "near the summit of an almost inaccessible hill, densely wooded from base to pinnacle, and interspersed with huge crags that appeared to tie loosely upon the soil, and in many cases were prevented from precipitating themselves into the valley's below, merely by the support of the trees against they were reclined. Deep ravines, in various directions, gave an air of still sterner solemnity to the scene."

Crags? Valleys? Ravines? Pinnacles? Why, there isn't even a real "mount" to Mount Pleasant, much less along the area abutting Rifle Range Road, where Poe's travelers would have landed.

At any rate, it is in this strange land that the famed "gold bug tree" was located. Contrary to popular belief, this wasn't an ancient oak, but a tulip tree—not the smallish tulip tree that blooms in spring favoring a magnolia blossom—but a large, deciduous tree, which can grow to tremendous heights.

Poe left the army and Fort Moultrie in 1829 to pursue his literary career. In 1845, *The Raven* followed *The Gold Bug* as a popular and immediate success. Wrote Poe, "The bird beat the bug, though, all hollow." Two other stories by Poe, *The Oblong Box* and *The Balloon Hoax* also use the Carolina coastline as settings. And some believe his poem, *Annabelle Lee*, was based on a lady from Charleston, the "kingdom by the sea."

Of course, Poe wrote *The Gold Bug* almost twenty years after his stay on Sullivan's Island. And, after all, the story is fiction. Or is it? It is entirely possible that, at some time in history, a pirate did bury treasure somewhere along our coast. Poe merely took the seed of a potential reality and converted it into a spectacular and dramatic story. Who knows? The ending may be buried right in your own back yard.

The Islands During
the Civil War

IN THIS PART OF THE country, the Civil War is better known as "The War Between the States" or "The War for Southern Independence." Even now, historians and laymen continue to debate this war—how it could happen that the newly formed and hard-fought United States of America, only seventy-years old, could erupt into such a bloody four-year conflict.

One thing that is rarely open to debate is the place where the war began. Ask almost anyone and they will answer, "Fort Sumter."

In essence, the war actually began on Sullivan's Island at Fort Moultrie when, on Christmas night 1860, the fort's commanding officer, Major Robert Anderson, decided to secretly evacuate that fort and remove his garrison to Fort Sumter, which was still unfinished at that time. It was an act seen by the South as rebellious and by the North as taking rightful possession of a United States military installation. Both arguments had merit. Sadly, there was no peaceful solution. The first shots, fired just before dawn on April 12, 1861, came from Morris Island and Fort Johnson on James Island. They were followed in short order by a barrage from Fort Moultrie on Sullivan's Island. The ultimate result was full-scale war.

"Martial law established on Sullivan's Island [and] the waters and marshes adjacent," reported the Charleston *Mercury* on February 9,

1861. Indeed, as hostilities grew, Sullivan's Island began to change from resort-island to active Confederate military post. In late March, Charleston merchant Jacob Frederic Schirmer, made this entry into his diary: "Nearly all the Houses on Sullivan's Island have been taken possession of by the Soldiers, Martial Law now there, and no one can go to the island without a permit from Genl. [Richard] Dunovant." As the war progressed, fortifications were erected across the island. Fort Moultrie, now strengthened, guarded the lower end of the island along with Battery Bee, built just below the fort in 1862. Battery Beauregard was erected in the middle section of the island while Battery Marshall overlooked Breach Inlet. All would be active participants during the four years of war as the Union repeatedly attempted to take Charleston.

To say that the island took a beating during the repeated battles for Charleston harbor is an understatement. In 1866, clergymen Charles Cotesworth Pinckney, Peter J. Shand and Paul Trapier wrote a report for the Episcopal Diocese of South Carolina concerning the destruction of churches during the war. They visited Grace Church, the Episcopal Church at Moultrieville. Their report graphically describes the island following the war and reads, in part: "when the houses on the island were removed to give place to those formidable batteries which, for four years, protected the harbor from hostile fleets, the Church was exposed to the chances of war. When the United States forces established their batteries on Morris Island, the Church then came in reach of their shells, which riddled roof and floor, and consumed the woodwork. Its roofless walls still lift up their solemn sides in the silence of the scene. Houses and population have both disappeared. The green earth-works with their frowning guns, cover the site of a once populous village—but you may walk their entire length without meeting soldier or citizen, or hearing any sound save the ceaseless roll of the sea."

The report closed with this heavyhearted addendum: "There is a strange and painful solitude reigning around those shores, where once our citizens flocked to stroll along the crowded beach; and a more solemn silence reigning over those massive works, whose thunders shook our city by day and night. Is this desolation the sure wages of war?"

Monumental Fort Sumter

The first thing that attracted the eye of the stranger, upon approaching Charleston from the sea, was Fort Sumter. It was built on an artificial island made of large blocks of stone. The walls were of dark brick and designed for three tiers of guns. The whole structure, as it rose abruptly out of the water, had a gloomy, prison-like appearance. It was situated on the edge of the channel, in the narrowest part of the harbor, between Fort Moultrie and Cummings Point, distant about a mile from the former place, and twelve hundred yards from the latter.

THIS DESCRIPTION OF FORT SUMTER was written by Abner Doubleday, second in command at the fort during its brief occupation by Union troops in early 1861. Today, Fort Sumter is one of the country's most historic and well-visited national monuments. Standing in the center of Charleston harbor and named for General Thomas Sumter, the "Gamecock" of Revolutionary War fame, the name "Sumter" would become permanently etched in America's memory for its historic role as the site of the "first shot" of the Civil War on April 12, 1861.

The genesis of Fort Sumter began much earlier, following the War of 1812. That conflict (especially the burning of Washington) showed the gross inadequacies of the Atlantic seaboard defenses. In 1815, President James Madison called for a new system of coastal defenses, but since the south Atlantic coast was considered "less important," it was not until 1826 that a report called for the erection of a fort in Charleston harbor. Only hindsight shows the shortsightedness of this original report, which glibly stated that building the fort would be "an easy and simple problem." Nothing could have been further from the truth.

Work began on the fort in 1829. Since it was to be built on nothing more than a sand bar in the harbor, known then as the "middle shoal," the first step was to strengthen the foundation. Work began with the placing of a pentagonally shaped ring of rocks around the base where the fort was to be erected.

Progress was slow. We're talking about hauling massive stones—tons of them—not just by land, but also by water. By 1834, five years after work began, this rock foundation or "mole," as it was called, was no more than two feet above low water and still open on one side to allow the supply ships to pass into the interior.

Then, in 1834, a land ownership dispute completely suspended operations. Charlestonian William Laval, with a grant showing that he owned 870 acres of "land" in Charleston harbor, laid claim to the site. Simultaneously, the South Carolina legislature launched an inquiry into whether "the creation of an Island on a shoal in the Channel, may not injuriously affect the navigation and commerce" of the harbor. Not only had the federal government begun work without consulting the state of South Carolina, but they had also done so without clearing a formal deed of land, believing it was unnecessary when that "land" was covered by water.

It wasn't until 1841 that these problems were cleared and work resumed, guided by Captain A.H. Bowman of the Corps of Engineers. Political issues and land ownership were replaced by the very real problems of building a fort in the middle of a channel with a rushing tidal flow. Bowman, however, was an engineering genius. He was a pioneer in understanding the natural give and take between man's use of land and the indomitable strength of the sea. One of his great achievements still stands at the south end of Sullivan's Island—the rock jetties on the south end of Sullivan's Island called Bowman's Jetty, known colloquially as the Grillage. In the 1840s these groins saved Sullivan's Island from erosion. They still do so today.

Under Bowman's guidance, work began in earnest. Bowman came up with a better, more durable way to lay the stone foundation, laying granite blocks in courses rather than using wooden timbers, which could rot, for a base. Still, problems abounded. There were times when the tides permitted no work at all. Periodic outbreaks of yellow fever suspended operations. Above all, there was the sheer magnitude of the task. Over 10,000 tons of granite, some of it brought all the way from Maine, had to be hauled in. Well over 60,000 tons of rock were imported from other sites. Bricks, shells and sand could be obtained locally, but the capacity of local brickyards was inadequate to supply the millions of bricks required to build the fort. Hundreds of thousands of oyster shells were required for the lime to make concrete. And transporting all of the above by water, against tides and weather, was a constant battle.

The Fort Sumter that Abner Doubleday described was an immense and imposing fortification. It stood fifty feet above the water, a five-sided, three-tiered fort designed to hold 135 guns. Its outer walls were five-feet thick. Inside, there was a parade ground of approximately one acre and three-story brick barracks for enlisted men. Along four walls were two tiers of arched gunrooms, while the fifth side, a 316.7-foot gorge, housed officers' quarters. In the center of this gorge was the sally port, which opened onto a 25 ½-foot-wide stone esplanade that extended the length of that wall onto a 171-foot wharf.

This massive, truly monumental task was never completely finished. In December 1860, when Union troops under Major Robert Anderson secretly occupied the fort on Christmas night, even after three decades and some seven million bricks later, the fort was still only 90 percent complete. The fort saw only four months of service in this near-complete state before the war began. Wrote Doubleday of the first bombardment, "Showers of balls . . . poured into the fort in one incessant stream, causing great flakes of masonry to fall in all directions. When the immense mortar shells, after sailing high in the air, came down in a vertical direction, and buried themselves in the parade ground, their explosion shook the fort like an earthquake." By the end of the war, Sumter was in ruins. It took thirty years to build Fort Sumter. It took four years to almost completely destroy this work.

Today, the fort is but a shadow of its original magnitude and what we see are the rebuilt remains of all that was left after the repeated bombardments of the Civil War. The fort lay dormant until the

1870s when there was a brief period of rebuilding and the outer walls, in ragged shambles, were leveled to approximately one-half of their original height. A new sally port was erected. This work halted in 1876 when a shortage of funds suspended operations. For twenty years the fort stood neglected except as a lighthouse station. It wasn't until 1898, and the onset of the Spanish-American War, that the fort was reactivated.

In 1899, Battery Huger was erected within the fort, named for Revolutionary War hero General Isaac Huger. Built in the central portion of the fort, this reinforced-concrete emplacement held a battery of 12-inch breech-loading guns. During World War II, this armament was replaced with 90-mm anti-aircraft guns. Finally, at the close of World War II, the fort was decommissioned. In 1948, Congress declared it a national monument. Less than one century after it gained fame as the starting place for America's most brutal conflict, Fort Sumter saw peace.

It took those rare qualities of engineering genius mixed with brute strength to build this great fort. It took only four years of an often-inhuman conflict to nearly destroy it. Still, the name "Sumter" lives on. People visit the fort annually from across the country and the world. They represent people from across the country and the world. Many have ancestors who fought in the Civil War, with both sides represented.

With due reverence, they come to pay homage to the fort's military past. Yet, equal respect is due those men instrumental in the design and erection of this truly great edifice. Those of us who live here see Fort Sumter constantly and a flicker of its place in history passes through our thoughts with every glance. Yes, we remember the war, the bombardments and the heroic struggles that took place within its brick walls. But next time you see the fort, look again. Remember those who built it. Fort Sumter is a place that lives in history as one of the great construction feats of all time.

Uncommon Valour: the *Keokuk* and the *Hunley*

"AMONG THE DARING AND SUCCESSFUL episodes of the Civil War," wrote Confederate engineer and historian John Johnson in 1890, "the recovery by the Confederates of the two guns from the wreck of the iron-clad vessel *Keokuk* deserves a place of the highest distinction."

Indeed. The USS *Keokuk* was one of the eight monitors involved in the failed Federal ironclad attack against Fort Sumter on April 7, 1863. Bravely, she had come closer to Sumter than any of her sister ships and, in so doing, received ninety hits. She limped away, finally sinking the following morning in eighteen feet of water off the southern end of Morris Island. The crew got out safely, but inside her twin steel-plated turrets were two huge cannons, powerful XI-inch Dahlgren smoothbores, and they were intact.

The cannons were formidable weapons of war, a prize the Federals hated to lose and the Confederates desperately needed, for they were mightier than any yet mounted in the defense of Charleston. In fact, you've likely seen one—it is the huge black cannon at White Point Gardens on the corner of South Battery and East Bay Street. The team of resourceful Confederates who salvaged this eight-ton weapon and its twin from the sunken *Keokuk* performed an incredible feat, as worthy of remembrance as the actions of the crew of the CSS *Hunley*. And, like the *Hunley*'s crew, the story of these men is one of bravery under seemingly impossible conditions.

If necessity is the mother of invention, when it came to innovation, the Confederate Navy was the matriarch. Outnumbered in manpower and machinery, facing the most formidable sea power in the word, the Secretary of the Confederate Navy had proclaimed that their only chance of success was through innovation. This eventually resulted in the superbly engineered *Hunley*, the semi-submersibles called the *Davids* and a remarkably advanced use of torpedo and mine warfare.

It was this very ingenuity, the creativity and skill of Confederate engineers, which rose to the surface in August 2000, with the excavation of the *Hunley*.

I was privileged to witness this historic event from the ringside seat of the press boat. What a gathering of emotions I felt as I watched the *Hunley* emerge from the deep, safe in its protective sling. Tears came when I saw that impossibly small hull and thought of the crewmen cramped inside and their death in its cold darkness. Yet I was simultaneously elated; I wanted to shout out a loud "hurrah!" And mingling with these profound feelings was an intense curiosity. What did she look like? How was she engineered? This was, perhaps, the biggest surprise of all. For here, preserved in far better condition than anyone thought possible, was a sleek and sophisticated invention, the stealth bomber of her time, possessing the shark-like configurations seen on submarines today.

The *Hunley* was after big prey. In 1863, the Federal blockading fleet off Charleston represented the greatest concentration of naval strength ever assembled. The flagship of this fleet was the steam-frigate *New Ironsides*. Armor-plated, manned by a crew of approximately 450 men and carrying sixteen guns, she was a 250-foot Goliath. The most powerful ship afloat, *New Ironsides* could fire a devastating broadside from eight 11-inch smoothbores. She was surrounded by dozens of support ships, including ironclads like the heavily armed *Keokuk* and warships like the eleven-gun steam-sloop *Housatonic*.

Which brings us back to the recovery of the *Keokuk*'s guns. Both Union and Confederate crews had independently pronounced them unsalvageable. General P.G.T. Beauregard, however, was not so easily discouraged. He sent his brilliant chief engineer, Major David B. Harris, out to the site with the indomitable General Roswell S. Ripley. The impossible mission was declared plausible. The work would have to be done in utmost secrecy, only at night, and only when the tide and seas were favorable. They would be working practically under the muzzles of the guns of the Federal fleet. It would take heroic determination mixed with the applied physics some call "thinking Egyptian."

Charlestonian Adolphus W. LaCoste of the army's ordnance department was placed in charge and his crew was hand picked for their expertise in moving heavy ordnance. The job was a mammoth task as enormous as the *Keokuk*'s sunken guns themselves. First, they had to remove the top of the *Keokuk*'s turrets—all armor plated—then enter the body of the ship itself. Here, working underwater, the crew needed to remove the massive bolts holding the cannons onto the gun carriages. Then they had to somehow raise the two 8-ton cannons and bring them back safely to Charleston.

These men had no diving bells or aqualungs. They had no underwater flashlights. The work was done in complete darkness and accomplished inch by inch and breath by breath, since the men, taking turns diving underwater, usually had only enough time to make one turn of a screw before they were forced to come up for air.

It took three weeks of this dangerous, excruciatingly slow, night work before the cannons were loose and in position to be hauled up. How LaCoste and his men would have wished for the powerful crane that later brought up the *Hunley*. Instead, LaCoste had ingeniously jury-rigged a large hulk, the former *Rattlesnake Shoals* lightship, turning it into a combination hoist and transport barge. Two huge twenty-foot timbers had been placed at the bow, fitted with hand-cranked lifting tackles. Approximately 1,500 sandbags balanced the vessel when the 8-ton gun was lifted from the water.

Slowly, the huge gun was hauled, butt-end up, until it was—almost—completely clear of the turret. The breech was free, but the tip of the muzzle was still inside the sunken boat. Thinking "Egyptian," LaCoste gave the order to move the sandbags to the back of the barge with hopes that the weight would lift the bow enough to free the cannon. The men also scrambled to the stern to add further weight. It wasn't enough. The muzzle was still inches inside the *Keokuk*.

And now the first streaks of dawn were showing on the horizon. They had run out of time. With daylight would come sure discovery by the Union patrol boats. It appeared that the effort was doomed. The only viable course of action was to order the lines holding the cannon cut and make a run for the harbor. LaCoste hesitated, wracking his brain for a solution.

Then fate, as a philosopher once stated, came "darkling down the torrent." Literally. During this pause, when all seemed lost, a large swell rolled in from the ocean. As it passed under the boat, it gently lifted the bow of the barge and, in an incredible instant, the cannon came free. Amidst muffled "hurrahs," LaCoste and his men tied the cannon fast, weighed anchor and made for the harbor, miraculously undetected by the Union patrol. Three nights later, the second gun was recovered without incident. One gun was placed at Battery Bee at Sullivan's Island, the other at Battery Ramsey at White Point Gardens, where it remains today.

Nerves of steel. Doing the impossible under impossible circumstances. Refusing to give up. LaCoste and his men were made of that indomitable fabric characterized by the quality called valor. These were no fools bent on a suicide mission. Neither was the crew of the *Hunley*. These were committed men putting brawn and brainpower together with the technology of the time to achieve an objective, despite the risk. Such is the way of war—all wars. Such is bravery. And such is the stuff of heroes.

Castle Pinckney

IT IS THE "OTHER" ISLAND in Charleston harbor, the one closest to peninsula Charleston and easily seen from the Battery, often mistaken by visitors for Fort Sumter. Although not much remains of Castle Pinckney proper, with its thick brick walls now crumbling amidst a tangle of wild vegetation, the site has a long and impressive history.

The actual name of this centrally located harbor island is "Shute's Folly." Like Folly Beach, the island, which was originally much larger, was named for the lush vegetation it once held ("folly" being an archaic term for a verdant thicket of trees and plants). The island's first historical mention is found in 1711 when its then-224 acres were deeded to Colonel Alexander Parris (for whom Parris Island near Beaufort was named), a commander of the South Carolina provincial militia. In 1746, the island was deeded to a Quaker named Joseph Shute, thus the name "Shute's Folly," and remained in the Shute family until 1763.

The island's history during these early years is sketchy, at best. Coastal Indians may have used it in some fashion, for old maps show circular formations of oyster shells, which may have been shell middens. As early as 1717, there is mention that the island was used as a place to hang convicted pirates, and legend has it that their bodies were left hanging from the gallows as a deterrent to others who might consider entering into acts of piracy. There is early mention of a grove of orange trees during the period of Shute's ownership and, indeed, during his time, oranges were grown in Charleston and the surrounding areas in some abundance. In 1805, fifty acres on the island were purchased by Jonathan Lucas, who, in 1795, had invented the first water-driven rice mill. Since maps of this period show a building on Lucas's property, it may be that he considered (or did) place a mill on the site.

Historically, the island's strategic harbor location gave it a military significance, yet throughout the centuries, the fort never quite attained full military importance. Even as early as 1736, when the first thought toward erecting a fortification on the island was considered, the intended fort was built instead at the point of Charleston's peninsula. It wasn't until the American Revolution that the first fort was erected on the island, and this was just a small earth and timber structure. In 1797, a second and somewhat larger fort was begun of logs and sand on the island. It was at this time that the fort was named to honor General Charles Cotesworth Pinckney of Revolutionary War fame. Facing southeast, this early fort was shaped in a half hexagon, mounted eight guns and held quarters for a small contingency of officers and men.

This fort was severely damaged by the hurricane of 1804, so much so that in 1808 the fort was entirely rebuilt, this time of brick, and constructed in a horseshoe shape. It mounted two tiers with a capability of holding twenty-one, possibly thirty guns and had quarters for 50 men in peacetime and 105 men when fully garrisoned. Despite the outbreak of the War of 1812, and Charleston's direct involvement in that conflict, the fort saw no action. By 1826, it was considered a "secondary" work by the defense department.

The island began to erode severely in the 1820s, causing further problems. In 1831, extensive repairs were necessary and stone embankments were put in place around the fort to offset the encroaching sea. It was maintained by a small garrison and housed a post hospital. With the outbreak of the Second Seminole War in 1835, the garrison was moved to Florida, and the fort was empty again.

It wasn't until the 1850s that Congress appropriated money to repair the fort, and in 1855 a navigation light was installed. Although the fort remained partially armed, it was ungarrisoned, and used primarily as a city powder storehouse. So it remained until 1860.

In December of that year, with secession fever at its height, preparations were made to re-garrison Castle Pinckney with U.S. troops. A lieutenant, an ordnance sergeant, four mechanics and thirty laborers were sent to clean up the fort. Following Major Robert Anderson's Christmas night move of his garrison from Fort Moultrie to Fort Sumter (a step seen by South Carolina as a direct act of war), on the afternoon of December 27, 1860, Castle Pinckney was taken, without incident, by a detachment from the 1st Regiment of Rifles under Colonel John J. Pettigrew. For the following four years, Castle Pinckney remained in Confederate hands.

Following the First Battle of Manassas (Bull Run) on July 21, 1861, Castle Pinckney was converted into a stockade for Union prisoners-of-war, garrisoned by the Charleston Zouave Cadets. During that battle, 130 Union soldiers were captured and held at the fort, including soldiers and officers from the 11th Zouaves, the 69th Irish Regiment, the 79th Highlanders, and the 8th Michigan Regiment. After their exchange in October, the fort was converted back to a defensive work, although its location in the inner harbor made it less strategically important than other harbor fortifications. By 1864, the fort's casemates were disarmed, the interior was filled with sand and although four guns remained on the island, it saw no further action. Following the Federal occupation of Charleston in February 1865, Castle Pinckney was again used for a brief time as a prison, primarily for captured blockade runners and civilian prisoners. This was probably the darkest part of Castle Pinckney's history, for it was during this period that twenty-five black Union soldiers who had participated in a mutiny were executed and buried on the island.

With peace, Castle Pinckney again fell into disuse. In 1878, with the island now under the control of the Treasury Department, a light station and supply depot was built on the island, at which time a light keeper's house and other buildings were erected. It remained active as a light station until 1917 when it was transferred to the U.S. Corps of Engineers who used the island buildings as a storage facility.

In 1924, President Calvin Coolidge designated Castle Pinckney as a National Monument, and it looked as if it might be preserved as an historical site. By 1933, however, when it came into the hands of the National Park Service, it was not considered "significant" enough to merit this status and was declassified. In 1958, it was sold to the South Carolina Ports Authority and, once again, plans for erecting a museum on the site were discussed. Again, nothing ever materialized. The island remained unoccupied and its buildings empty. Finally, in December 1967, a tremendous fire broke out on the island, a blaze that destroyed the house and other wooden buildings on the island.

Today, Castle Pinckney is on the National Register of Historic Places and is owned by the Sons of Confederate Veterans, Fort Sumter Camp 1269. There is hope that someday the site will be fully explored historically and archaeologically, and what remains of the original fort preserved. Let us hope that this work soon comes to pass, for Castle Pinckney holds an unquestionably important place in Charleston's past. Until then, it remains an abandoned, silent sentinel in Charleston's harbor of history.

Skirmish on Bull's Island

JANUARY 1863 WAS A PERIOD of marked activity in the waters contingent to Charleston harbor. Up to this point, the swift and daring blockade runners had been enjoying, despite the blockade, a remarkable success. Yet in January, the tide turned. Union vessels had seized the *Mercury, Florida, Pride, Etiwan, Emma Tittle* and *Princess Royal.* Washington promised four more gunboats and also the most powerful ship in the U.S. Navy at that time, the USS *New Ironsides.*

The Confederates were doing everything in their power to break the blockade. On January 30, action in the Stono River led to the capture of the Federal steamer *Isaac Smith* by an expedition under Colonel Joseph A. Yates of the first South Carolina Artillery. On January 31, Confederate gunboats *Chicora* and *Palmetto*, under Commodore Duncan N. Ingraham, made an astounding sneak attack on the blockading fleet off the Charleston bar, leaving two Union ships disabled and driving the remaining fleet offshore. This daring feat opened the Charleston bar for twenty-four hours.

It is against this backdrop of events that a small Confederate scouting party from Battery Marshall on Sullivan's Island and Federal servicemen from the Union gunboat *Flambeau* met accidentally on Bull's Island.

Bull's Island is the largest and northernmost of the string of barrier islands that run from Cape Romain south to Charleston harbor. Ostensibly, the men from the USS *Flambeau* were on a hunting expedition when they met up with the Confederate scouts.

Accounts of this accidental encounter are presented by each side in a report filed by the officers in charge, Lieutenant Commander Upshure of the USS *Flambeau* and Captain Charles T. Haskell, First South Carolina (regular) Infantry. These reports are found in Series I, Volume XIII, pages 573-4, of the Official Records of the War of the Rebellion.

The following is a report from Lieutenant Commander Upshure to Rear Admiral S.F. DuPont, commanding the South Atlantic Blockading Squadron:

(Off Bull's Island, February 2, 1863) SIR: I have to report the capture of Acting Master William B. Sheldon and Acting First Assistant Engineer A.G. Pemble, the wounding of Acting Ensign G. Cottrell, and the killing, I fear, of Alexander Cushman, Captain of the foretop, all of this vessel, under the following circumstances.

On the morning of the 31st ultimo Officers Sheldon and Pemble landed on Bull's Island for the purpose of foraging, my clerk, Mr. d'Estimauville, accompanying the latter and a contraband the former. At noon, Messrs. Pemble and d'Estimauville, while approaching the Negro quarters of a plantation, known as Gibbes' farm, had their suspicions aroused by seeing smoke issued from one of the chimneys. At the same instant ten men, commanded by an officer, filed out of the dwelling, distant about 20 yards. They were well dressed in Confederate uniforms and armed with short rifles and pistols. Believing their capture imminent, Mr. d'Estimauville proposed the expedient of flight and at once started, but Mr. Pemble, believing himself unseen, dropped into the bushes close by. Meanwhile three of the enemy gave chase to Mr. d'Estimauville, calling to him, 'Surrender, or we'll fire!' but that officer, relying on his speed to elude them, continued on his course. After running about a mile and a half and finding that only one of his pursuers was gaining on him, he turned and fired his rifle, apparently with some effect, as the Confederate dropped his piece and suddenly halted. The two others still continued the chase, but Mr. d'Estimauville gained cover and, lying perdu until they had passed, escaped them. He subsequently succeeded in reaching the vessel.

About 2 p.m. Mr. Sheldon and the contraband arrived at the same farm and were almost immediately surrounded. Five or six rifles bore directly on Mr. Sheldon and he, seeing resistance vain, necessarily surrendered. The contraband, however, was more fortunate, and though five shots were fired at him on his flight, he reached the ship in safety and gave us the information. I at once got the ship under way and, proceeding as far inland as possible, dispatched an adequate force to recapture the missing officers.

After a search of four hours, which I regret to say was ineffectual, no traces of the enemy being visible, the boats returned to the ship about 11 p.m.

Still hoping to find Mr. Pemble, on the following morning I sent another expedition to scour that part of the island. The detachment under command of Lieutenant Smith landed, and throwing out skirmishers as they advanced, cautiously examined Gibbes' farm, and were proceeding toward the summerhouse, a mile and half distant and in partial view, when the advance came across the pistol worn the previous day by Mr. Pemble, the gun which Mr. Sheldon had used, and other objects evidently left by the enemy as a decoy, and which it was to be regretted our officers did not have the foresight to appreciate in time.

About a mile from Gibbes' farm the road lay over an embankment and through a dense undergrowth. Here the enemy were in ambush, and as Ensign Cottrell and Mr. d'Estimauville, with their skirmishers, advanced on the place they were received with a volley of about twenty balls, succeeded by a scattered fire of as many more. My coxswain and Cushman, captain of the foretop, were within 10 yards of the enemy, and Cushman fell mortally wounded, I fear. Mr. Cottrell received two wounds, one in the muscle of the left arm and the other through the fleshy part of the right thigh, neither of which the surgeon regards as serious. The enemy being completely invisible and evidently in force, Lieutenant Smith prudently withdrew and embarked his men in good order and without further casualties. The enemy never once broke cover.

As the sequel proves, it was imprudent to permit our officers and men to go so far from the ship, but the impunity with which parties from the Restless, and lately from this vessel, have traversed the island has engendered an overconfidence on our part, and I may as well state that a recurrence of the disaster will be carefully avoided for the future.

Report of Captain Charles T. Haskell Jr. CSA, commanding Battery Marshall, from Sullivan's Island to Captain W. F. Nance, Assistant Adjutant-General, First Military District, CSA:

(BATTERY MARSHALL, S.C. February 3, 1863.) SIR: For the purpose of preparing to carry out orders issued to me, I left Sullivan's Island on the afternoon of January 30 with seven men and landed at Gibbes' house on Bull's Island that evening about dark. I spent the next morning in exploring the different creeks back of the island, and was just proceeding to reconnoiter the position of the gunboat Flambeau lying near when I met with and captured a man calling himself the chief engineer of the Flambeau. He was armed with an Enfield rifle and a navy revolver, but said he was only out on a shooting expedition. I sent him off in my boat to the west end of the island, and, supposing that he had companions, concealed myself and fired off his gun to entice them. Another man soon came up with a Negro. I took the former prisoner, but the Negro ran away. The man professed to be a second lieutenant and acting master of the Flambeau; was armed with a musket and gave the

same account of himself as the first. I hurried him off to the west end of the island and sent both to Sullivan's Island, sending at the same time to ask that 50 men should be sent me.

I remained at the island that night, and about sunset the Flambeau came around to within a quarter of a mile of Gibbes' house, and coming to anchor within 200 yards of the island, set from 100 to 120 men ashore. They advanced a short distance, searched Gibbes' settlement, and went aboard again. I slept at Gibbes' house that night, and the next morning the 50 men who I had desired to be sent me arriving at the west end of the island, I immediately advanced, being anxious to lie in ambush at Gibbes' Wharf. The distance, however, was about 4 miles, and by the time I had passed over half of it I was met by one of my scouts, who informed me that the enemy had landed and were advancing. Directly afterwards I saw them myself, about 75 men in front, with a reserve of about 20 more about 500 yards farther back. They were marching through an open field in close order. I formed my men (45, the rest having been left in the boats) just back of Gibbes' summerhouse, and as they came up they gave them a volley from half of my force, ordering the remainder to reserve their fire, as I expected them to charge me. It seemed to take them by surprise, as they had not yet seen me, and they immediately retreated in confusion, returning my fire as they went. The very dense thicket prevented my fire from being very effective. They left one man dead on the ground; a first lieutenant of marines, commanding the detachment, was apparently mortally wounded, and another man also appeared to be wounded. I knew that they had a launch with a rifled gun in it, with which they could destroy my boats and cut off my retreat, and having only one day's rations, I considered it best to cross over to Capers Island and wait for reenforcements. I accordingly, after waiting for them to renew the attack about half an hour, marched back to my boats and crossed over the inlet dividing the two islands, sending off a boat at the same time to ask for reenforcements.

I waited on Caper's Island until the next evening at 8 o'clock, when I received orders to return to Sullivan's Island. I set out at 9 o'clock and arrived at this post early this morning.

I am sir, very respectfully, your obedient servant, CHARLES T. HASKELL, JR.

The Moultrie House

IT WAS A STATELY AND elegant hotel, standing beachfront just to the east of Fort Moultrie, offering a glorious view of Charleston harbor and the ocean. It was the pride of Moultrieville and, in the 1850s, it was *the* place to see and be seen during the hot, Lowcountry summer months.

"I never saw anything like it before," wrote William Gilmore Simms through his fictional character, Tom Appleby, in the whimsical short story, "Flirtation at the Moultrie House." "The supper tables were glorious, feeding eye and appetite at the same time, to the great satisfaction of both. Think of the oysters alone costing more than forty dollars and you will have some notion of all the rest . . . The wines were in great profusion, and the popping of champagne was as frequent as that of musketry at the battle of San Jacinto. We did not break up till three in the morning, and then a dozen of us took to the beach, and stripping for the sea, had a glorious buffeting for twenty minutes in the breakers."

Designed by architect Edward C. Jones and built at a cost of $32,000, the hotel officially opened on July 8, 1850, and boasted luxurious accommodations for two hundred people. "Its frame is of yellow pine supported on brick piers," wrote one of Charleston's favored historians of that period, Dr. John B. Irving. "The building proper, is 256 feet long and 40 feet wide, with wings at end 100 feet long, 35 feet wide, with front piazza 16 feet wide, and back piazza 10 feet wide. This central portion of the building projects in front, and continues up through the roof, forming an attic of two stories. Its situation, too is most judicious, commanding an inspiring view of the Harbour and Bay of Charleston, and of the Sea . . . the surf of which dashes up on a wide beach, not many feet from the Hotel, and then breaks into little billows, which as, if instinct with life, keep continually chasing each other like children in play far up on the sand."

The Moultrie House soon gained a national reputation as a luxury resort, known for providing the finest foods and "no deficiency of amusements," including four billiard tables, three bowling saloons, horses for riding, boats for fishing and "none but the choicest liquors." The first floor was designed so that the east wing held a succession of spacious rooms linked by large folding doors which, when opened, formed a 110-foot grand ballroom. Throughout the summer season, this ballroom saw a constant succession of balls, musicals, teas and masques—a place both popular and notorious for its "flirtations." "I have half fallen in love with one of the Charleston girls," wrote the fictional Tom Appleby, "as fair as a lily and gentle as a zephyr. But no more of this. It may be after all, nothing but a flirtation. This is a famous place for flirtation, I find, and the practice, which might worry a too earnest fellow, has nevertheless, something very graceful and pleasant in it."

On the western wing was a commodious dining room, spacious at ninety feet by twenty-eight feet and airy with tall, multi-paned, floor-to-ceiling windows. To the rear of the building were the kitchens and two large cisterns, which furnished the house with water. Here was also a large bathroom for the ladies, with water supplied via windmill.

Since the Moultrie House catered to the upper crust, every detail was considered to make their stay enjoyable. One indulgence was the "Moultrieville Rail and Plank Company," a short horse-drawn railway which ran from the ferry landing at the Cove to the hotel. After disembarking, passengers would then board horse-drawn rail cars and be carried directly to the hotel's front door. Heaven forbid that a lady or gentleman might dirty a slipper by stepping on the sand!

The following advertisement appeared in the *Charleston Courier on* June 25, 1854 and describes some of the grandeur that visitors could expect from the Moultrie House:

This elegant summer retreat haven been opened for the reception of visitors for the season, the proprietor respectfully informs his numerous friends and the public generally that nothing on his part shall be left undone to afford comfort and gratification to all who may favor him with their company. The weekly "Hops" that gave so much satisfaction last season, will be continued, an efficient band of music having been engaged for that purpose. Steamboats leave the City and Island throughout the day at convenient hours. Conveyances run to and from each boat—fare 12 ½ cents, and commodious carriages can be obtained by applying at the office, by those desirous of enjoying a drive on the magnificent beach. Dinner will be on the table every day at 4 p.m., except Sundays, when the hour will be 2:30 p.m. Families and others desiring apartments will please address THOMAS A. NICKERSON, Mills House, Charleston, S.C. where a box will be kept for the reception of letters, parcels, &. intended for the visitors at the Moultrie House, the contents of which will be forwarded by each boat.

Luxury notwithstanding, the main purpose for "resorting" to the island was to escape the deadly diseases which plagued the city and area plantations during the summer. Yet even the "salubrious" breezes, which so favored the island, could not keep the Moultrie House immune from a fever outbreak in 1858. Shortly after completing medical school, young John Safford Stoney spent the summer on the island. In his *Recollections of John Safford Stoney, Confederate Surgeon,* he wrote,

I went down to Sullivan's Island and took rooms in the Moultrie House, then kept by Daniel Mixon of the Charleston Hotel, and stuck up my shingle for the practice of medicine. I had a very pleasant time, going to two or three dances each week at the hotel and at private houses. I enjoyed a very fair practice until in July, when Yellow Fever was brought over from Charleston and several deaths occurred at the hotel. There was a perfect stampede and in several days the hotel was deserted and closed up. I then moved to my aunt's, Mrs. FitzSimmons, in whose family I had several cases of fever. Old Dr. Horlbeck and Professor Julian Chisolm having gone North, they turned over their patients to me, and until October when the season of the Island closed I had enjoyed the largest practice on the Island.

The glory days of the Moultrie House came to an abrupt halt in 1861 as Sullivan's Island turned from resort to Confederate military post. The hotel, now used as housing for Confederate officers, made a ready target for Union bombardments. Union officer Abner Doubleday was stationed at Fort Sumter during the bombardment of April 12, 1861, the first action of the war. "Since the rebel occupation of Fort Moultrie, this hotel had been used as a depot and barracks for the troops in the vicinity," he later wrote in his book *Reminiscences of Forts Sumter and Moultrie in 1860-61.* "I . . . aimed 2 forty-two pounder balls at the upper story. The crashing of the shot, which went through the whole length of the building among the clapboards and interior partitions, must have been something fearful to those who were within. They came rushing out in furious haste, and tumbled over each other until they reached the bottom of the front steps, in one writhing, tumultuous mass."

Following the Union surrender of Fort Sumter, Doubleday was asked why he had fired on a civilian building. "Not caring to enter into a discussion at that time, I evaded it by telling him . . . the landlord had given me a wretched room there one night, and this being the only opportunity that had occurred to get even with him, I was unable to resist it. He laughed heartily and said, 'I understand it all now. You were perfectly right, sir, and I justify the act.' "

There was a brief period following the war when attempts were made to re-establish the Moultrie House to its former grandeur, but times had changed. Gone were the great antebellum days of wealthy plantation owners seeking elegant surroundings in which to spend the summer season. Today, no vestige remains of this once-great hotel and the site has reverted back to tall dunes and heavy thickets and myrtle groves. But in the 1850s it was one of the grandest hotels on the entire eastern seaboard—the place of choice for those who wished to "combine comfort with pleasure" in exquisite and impeccable style.

Fishing in 1850

"I F FISH KEEP NIBBLING AT bait, they must expect, at last to get a hook in their gills," asserted nineteenth-century writer and historian, Dr. John Beaufain Irving. He was describing a fishing excursion, taken in 1850 from Sullivan's Island, in a monograph called *Local Events and Incidents at Home*, a somewhat glorified collection of "things to do" on and around the islands. The piece was basically an advertisement for the Moultrie House, the grand and immensely popular hotel on Sullivan's Island at that time. Dr. Irving was no seasoned fisherman; otherwise he would have known that a fish takes the bait in its mouth, not the gills. Still, despite Dr. Irving's often-florid style, he was a good storyteller, a requisite for any angler.

Bless me! what a bite—jerked is the line, but the fellow is off—why what a voracious rascal! 'I have him,' says another of our crew, and sure enough with better luck, he drags him to the surface—why, it is a young shark—how he resists with determined energy every effort made to haul him out of the water—his fins are busily at work with immense power, beating the water by his side, like the paddles of a small steamer, but he is finely hooked, and he cannot tear himself loose—with one tremendous flirt, however, just as he is about to be dragged into the boat, he severs the line, as if it was a cambrick thread, breaks away, and disappears from our sight, soon to sport again in the depths of his native element!

Now, we have another nibble; what a contrast to the last voracious rascal. This is some lazy little fellow, or dainty gentleman, that must needs taste the dish offered to him, before he ventures to devour it. He finds it a more tempting morsel than he at first anticipated, for he has laid hold, and up he comes—he seems angry, however, at the liberty taken with him, in being dragged so unceremoniously from his quiet bed, for he is croaking, and making a great noise, complaining as it were at our unfeeling conduct, as we drop him into the basket.

Dr. Irving's complaining croaker was taken from a boat anchored at Dewees Inlet between Isle of Palms and Dewees Island. Like any inlet, the location offered superb fishing for a variety of species. It is as popular a fishing spot today as it was in 1850. The "Shark Hole," a hole eighty feet deep, located where the inlet meets the Intracoastal Waterway, is noted for its excellent fishing, particularly shark fishing.

"The common mode of fishing in our waters is with a plumb line," wrote Irving, "a flat piece of lead placed on a line about a foot from the hooks, which are generally three in number, two swinging from each side of the lead, and one attached about six inches above it. The line thus weighted, enables the fisherman to throw his line to a reasonable distance, and as soon as it reaches the bottom, it is gradually drawn along, so as to keep up a gentle motion, by which the bait is continually in attractive action, inviting the attention of the fish it is intended to victimize. Shrimp is the bait preferred and commonly used when procurable, but other expedients have to be resorted to at different seasons."

One of the first to popularize the use of the rod and reel in salt water fishing was none other than the great Confederate hero and South Carolina governor, General Wade Hampton Jr., whose plantation was Woodlands, near Columbia. Hampton was vacationing on Sullivan's Island at the same time as Dr. Irving, who was duly impressed by Hampton's fishing acumen. Wrote Irving, "WADE HAMPTON, JR., who is now on a visit to our sea shore for a few weeks, known as one of the most indefatigable and accomplished anglers of his day surprized us, by using a rod and reel with great success. It is quite amusing to see the astonishment . . . as Hampton gracefully throws his line the distance of many feet, and as soon as he gets a bite, from large or small fish, lifts him into his basket with unerring skill."

Hampton, who Dr. Irving called a "real disciple of old Isaac Walton," was using a pole made of long cane, or Santee cane, *seasoned and prepared in a particular manner, to give them pliancy and strength, for the purpose of fishing. We understand there is a particular mode of seasoning these canes, known only to a few persons, and to which process, when the cane is subjected, it has no longer any brittle properties, but it becomes most enduring and elastic. . . . A Negro fellow belonging to Col. Hampton, at the Woodlands in Columbia, possesses the secret, as to the process by which these canes are prepared, but he cannot be induced to divulge it. The process is a very slow one, requiring two years to complete. The cane Hampton uses, was taken from the swamps of the Congaree River, and was prepared by the fellow we have alluded to, and we presume will hold any fish, that human power, aided by human skill, can control.*

To illustrate the point, Irving tells this story:

Hampton . . . was exceedingly ambitious on his first arrival among us, to capture a Shark, which he maintained he would be able to do with his rod and line, with as much ease, as was generally accomplished by a hand line. He had not been out fishing many times, before his wish was gratified. . . . His line had been thrown out, as usual, several feet, and had reached the bottom. It had not been there many minutes, 'When he was sure . . . He felt a bite, but ne'er had felt before.' From the first tug, it seemed as if there could be no escape for the daring adventure—he was firmly hooked—when Hampton relying upon the goodness of his tackle and his skill, did not think it even worth while to play him, in the hope of first tiring him out, but at once boldly began to take in his line. Steadily he handled his rod. Soon through the clear water, could be traced, as he approached the boat, the dark outline of the animal. As he catches a glimpse of us, he turns and tries to be off, but not being able to make good his retreat, he flounders and whips the waves in very madness, trying to escape his doom. The reel is loosened for a moment, and we hear its music, like the hum of many bees, but only for a moment—it is again silent, and wound up gradually. After a few more minutes spent in splashing, flouncing and flapping on the surface of the water, by a dexterous exercise of gentle violence, he is expertly whipt out of the sea—for a second he is seen dangling in the air, and then he is triumphantly lodged in the bottom of the boat.

The shark was measured and weighed and was reported to be four feet long, weighing twenty pounds. "A small Shark," wrote Irving, "when compared with some we have seen caught in our harbour, but yet very large to be captured in the manner we have described."

After Irving's fishing excursion, his party "repaired to the Club House, a rude though comfortable hut, constructed for the accommodation of fishing parties upon the borders of the inlet, where we were fishing, a fire was lighted, and the best of our fish, selected for our repast, fresh out of the water, were cooked artistically in the boiling fat of good sweet pork. They were handed to us hot from the frying pan, and eaten with a relish and appetite, which needed no artificial sauce to heighten it—in fact, it is always readily admitted that no fish taste so well and are so much enjoyed as those we catch ourselves, and eat in company with boon companions by the water side."

The Grillage

Some of the best flounder and sheephead fishing in South Carolina is found around the rocks at the southern end of Sullivan's Island in front of Fort Moultrie, a spot popularly known as the "Grillage." Even if you aren't a fisherman, the view from this picturesque setting is splendid, offering an up-close look at historic Fort Sumter and, in the distance, the steepled skyline of downtown Charleston. Porpoises can almost always be spied feeding in the currents swirling around the rocks and there is no better vantage point for watching ships coming in or out of the harbor.

Obviously, South Carolina is not known for its rocky shores. When were these rocks put there, and why?

The Grillage dates back to the 1840s when, after a series of severe storms and hurricanes, the south end of Sullivan's Island began to seriously erode. At extreme tides, waves were actually washing against the sides of Fort Moultrie. The task of halting this erosion was given to Captain Alexander H. Bowman of the U.S. Army Corps of Engineers, a man of true genius who should be honored for achieving what may have been the first successful coastal zone planning in South Carolina history.

A "grillage," by definition, is a framework of timbers on which rocks are placed to act as a breakwater. Bowman's first grillage was erected parallel to the shoreline and although it worked in the short run, he soon discovered that the *parallel* placement of rocks on a sandy beach eventually accelerated erosion. The currents were doing nothing more than undermining the sand beneath the rocks.

After careful study, Bowman correctly concluded that there was a prevalent north-south drift to the offshore current along the Carolina shoreline. He then erected his next stone jetty *perpendicular* to the shore; his theory being that the sand washed by the currents would be caught by the rocks, and eventually build up on the beach.

Bowman's plan worked. Within one year, "Bowman's Jetty" had accreted the beach at the lower end of Sullivan's Island by almost two hundred feet.

Bowman's Jetty worked wonders in saving the south end of Sullivan's Island, and still does. During the Civil War, however, a rock jetty jutting out into the entrance to Charleston harbor played havoc with Confederate vessels running the Union blockade. At that time, the main channel was on the south side of the harbor by Morris Island, but that side of the harbor held a flotilla of armed Union vessels. The Sullivan's Island channel was protected by the Confederate guns at Fort Moultrie and was obviously preferable. Bowman's Jetty, however, made this run unpredictable and dangerous. If a ship hugged the Sullivan's Island shore too closely she could hang up on the rocks. Many did.

The British steamer *Minho* was one of the first to wreck there while attempting to make the run into the harbor in October 1862. Underwater archaeologist Dr. E. Lee Spence, in his book on blockade running, *The Real Rhett Butler & Other Revelations*, noted that the cargo salvaged from the *Minho* not only included basic commodities such as coffee, sugar, matches, candles, spices, sardines, cigars and cigar lighters, but also "303 cases of assorted brandies, 156 cases of claret, gin, whiskey and assorted wines, 221 cases of champagne, 25 barrels of bottled ale and 12 barrels of bottled port." Even in the grips of war, Southerners kept a taste for the high life and blockade runners were more than willing to take the risks necessary to procure these luxuries. Even basics like salt and sugar went for exorbitantly high prices. One can only imagine what a case of champagne was worth.

The French steamer *Renaudin* went ashore at Bowman's Jetty on February 23, 1863, but was successfully got off the following day. Not so lucky was the Confederate steamer, *Stono*. While attempting to run out of the harbor with a load of cotton on June 5, 1863, she was chased back into the harbor by the Federal gunboat *Wissahicken*, eventually wrecking on Bowman's Jetty. The *Stono* had seen a short life as a blockade runner. This vessel, which had started the war as the Union gunboat *Isaac P. Smith*, had been captured by the Confederates in the Stono River on January 30, only three months earlier.

The propeller steamer *Prince Albert*, bound for Nassau, was on her third run through the blockade when she ran aground at Bowman's Jetty on August 9, 1864, possibly hanging up on the wreck of the *Minho*. The *Flamingo*, described as a beautiful, black, side-wheel paddle steamer, had made numerous successful runs through the blockade when she finally wrecked near Bowman's Jetty on October 23, 1864. A little over a month later, the *Beatrice*, coming in from Nassau, ran ashore near the wreck of the *Flamingo* while trying to enter the harbor under heavy shelling from the Union fleet.

The last blockade runner to be claimed by the Grillage was the *Celt*, which ran into Bowman's Jetty on February 14, 1865, as she was leaving Charleston with a "valuable cargo of cotton." Ironically, this side-wheel steamer wrecked the day before Union forces occupied Charleston and it was the Yankees who benefited from the *Celt's* salvaged cargo.

The Grillage also claimed ships of war. On January 12, 1865, the iron-plated Confederate ram, USS *Columbia*, ran onto a sunken wreck in this vicinity but luckily was able to save her crew by running the ship aground on Sullivan's Island. Three days later the Federal monitor, USS *Patapsco*, hit a Confederate mine laid between Fort Sumter and Sullivan's Island. Tragically, even though she was only 1,200 yards off Fort Moultrie, 64 of her 105 crewmembers died. A monument erected in their honor now stands at the entrance to Fort Moultrie next to Osceola's grave.

Even today the Grillage can claim lives. This may be a beautiful place to view the harbor and is still a great fishing spot, but the currents swirling around the rocks and their proximity to the shipping channel make this an exceptionally dangerous place to swim. Despite large signs warning visitors of deep holes and treacherous currents, someone invariably ignores the warnings and goes in—for the last time.

   Ah, but one does not need to wet a toe to cast a fishing line here to savor a magnificent sunset over Charleston's harbor. The Grillage is an exceptional place of beauty and has been eyewitness to a remarkable history. Let the lives it has claimed remain in the past. Enjoy it—but stay out of the water.

A Description of the Island in 1858

T HE REPORTER OF THE FOLLOWING *News & Courier* article from August 12, 1858, wrote an exceptionally good description of Sullivan's Island in antebellum days. She (or he) wrote anonymously as "Rosamond" and was staying at the elegant Moultrie House Hotel.

For the information of my numerous friends and comrades of the "Can't get away Club," whose traveling experience is restricted to the limits of "the vicinity," I have taken up my pen to give you some items concerning this attractive home resort.

From the ferry wharf at the foot of Market-street, the little steamer Osiris makes five trips per day to the Island, in accordance with the following schedules, which is understood to meet the attraction wants of a large majority of residents and visitors. . . .

At each arrival of the boat the cars of the Mixerville and Moultrieville Rail Road, propelled by horse (and mule) power, appear in sight or in waiting, on which the traveler is conveyed for ten cents to any point along the line of road. The route lies through Middle-street, passing all the churches, the fort, and other objects of interest, to the Depot adjoining the Hotel. The cars remain at each stopping place sufficiently long to land passengers and baggage, with despatch. Traversing thus the center of the village of Moultrieville, we have an opportunity of noting all points of any whatever, and I shall now proceed briefly to describe them.

Immediately at the Cove, in a very open situation, is the old Planters Hotel, for many years kept by Mrs. Cheney, and now under the direction of Mrs. Gidire, which, we learn, has been well patronized throughout the present season. In the vicinity is a nest of cottages, used as bar rooms and lounging places, which a little enterprise and public spirit might soon convert into neat, comfortable cottages, forming a nucleus for the erection and establishment of a good hotel or first class boarding house, embracing all the advantages of proximity to the landing and the enjoyment of the sea breeze in profusion, being open to the wind from whatever direction it may come. On the left is Mrs. Fitzsimon's, the oldest established boarding house, I believe, on the Island, which entrances from the back beach and Middle-street. A little farther on is the Episcopal Church, venerable structure, which has stood the test of many gales, and afforded to the benighted and houseless a temporary refuge from the storm. It is considered the safest retreat, next to the fort itself, which the Island affords, in such contingencies. This Church is regularly opened for public worship, under the Rectorship of Rev. E. T. Walker. Its accommodations have been enlarged from time to time, but the congregation is so large and increasing that there is still but little spare room beyond the pews rented by permanent worshippers.

As we proceed there is but little or no evidence of encroachment upon the primitive style and character of the architecture, or the habits and customs of the people. An exception, however, to this remark may be noticed in the recently erected and tasteful resident of Mr. Wm. Curtis, planned and built by him, as I am informed, for a permanent sea-side home. Mr. Gilliland's spacious house, next to the Presbyterian Church is also an indication that there are some enterprising capitalists who are disposed to inaugurate an improved condition of things. This delightful location is now occupied by the Misses Mitchell, as a Boarding House. Ladies who have stopped here, speaking the most enthusiastic manner of the comfort, convenience and coolness of the apartments, the courteous and accommodating spirit of the hostesses, and the indefatigable attentions and civilities of the servants and all connected with the establishment. Having tested all these things in my own person, I can readily bear testimony to all that they say about it. . . .

A little farther on, the fine, commodious residences of the Messrs. ADGER, FARRAR, GILLILAND and a few others, command our attention, as additional innovations upon the old styles of building, and the examples of these enterprising gentlemen, seem to have had their effect upon some of their neighbors, who are beginning to wake up to the necessity and importance of enlarging their accommodations. For it is an old and venerable custom on this Island, for town folks to be very regular and punctual in coming down spend a few weeks sociably with "dear friends," from whom unforeseen circumstances have unfortunately separated them all the previous winter, though living in the same city, perhaps within a few squares. And it is wise and prudent in our Islanders to make more ample provision every year for their accommodation, as these "summer friends" invariably increased in number with each returning "watering season."

Now we are at the Fort, upon and around which are gathered multitudes of children and nurses, and a bright array of fair faces and fairy forms. Every eye is lighted up with enjoyment, for this merry throng have evidently been listening to the enchanting strains of sweet music from the fort Band (considered one of the best in the Army.) This portion of the Island is a fashionable afternoon resort, and it is well worth a visit to Moultrieville to mingle for an hour or tow with the happy crowd as-sembled on the parade ground.

Opposite the Fort is the Quarter-Master's Office—the upper room of which is appropriated to religious services, in the forenoon of every Sunday, by the Chaplain, Rev. Mr. Harris, to which the Islanders and visitors are invited. At another corner is the rural looking residence, formerly of M. C. Mordecai, now owned by Mr. Benjamin Mordecai. Here the eye, grievously oppressed with the glare of sandbanks innumerable, is relieved with the welcome refreshment of nature's brightest green, the house being completely embowered in foliage and shrubbery, and the spacious lot enclosed with a neat white paling fence, presenting a very pretty contrast of delicate hues. It has been suggested that the large open space between this corner and the Fort, might, before the opening of another season, be converted into an enclosed public square, covered into an enclosed public square, covered with a green award, and planted with suitable trees, answering the purpose of a grand gathering-place for the ladies, a play-ground for the children, ice-cream garden, &c. ala White Point. And it is worthy the consideration of the authorities and of the property holders and residents of the Island, whether as important a measure of improvement might not be accomplished by a generous co-operation, and an appeal to the Government for aid, though the medium of a generally subscribed memorial to that effect.

We have not reached the upper end of the Island, and after catching a passing glimpse of the tasteful modern residences of Gen. Martin, Rev. Mr. Drayton, Messrs. Howard, Stenmeyer, and others, on the front beach, are coming in full view of Mixer's Grand Palace, with its magnificent piazzas looking out on the broad open sea, its capacious saloons and cool apartments, fanned with the delicious breezes of old Ocean, groups of promenaders within, without, around, and on the beach, presenting the most lively spirit-stirring scene imaginable, the very sight of which makes the drooping heart rebound, and the dejected, worn-out body becomes invigorated and clothed with a new existence. Certain significant indications of unusual commotion among the guests, remind the new-coming that this is "Hop Night," a regular weekly reunion of the votaries of Terpsichore, which has become part and parcel of the ar-rangements of the Hotel, and attracts scores of both sexes and all conditions of people from the City and Island, either in the capacity of actors or spectators.

Supper over, the early part of the evening is devoted to walking, riding, and promenading parties, and dressing for the Hop, which generally begins and drags its slow length along between 9 and 10 o'clock, while the dancers and lookers on are coming in by degrees, and taking their positions in the drawing rooms, or (what is decidedly more comfortable and pleasant) in the piazzas overlooking them. If you "don't Dance," or your dancing days or over, or you are ugly, and your papa has no plantation . . . and you are afraid of being "a wall flower," you choose the latter alternative, and therein show your wisdom, for being afflicted with all the aforementioned qualifications, I have tried it, and am satisfied with the result. I am, as you may probably guess, one of those unfortunates called "slow people," who are behind the age, and like to stay behind the scenes, and look on. Luckily, however, I have fallen in with a part as "slow" as myself, and not given to late hours. So while the beaux and belles are still "tripping it on the light fantastic toe," down stairs, we snatch a favorable opportunity to take almost exclusive possession of the lofty promenade overhead, and listening to the music of the saloon, blending harmoniously with the music of the waves, bid defiance to Morpheus, until the watching hour of midnight whispers "bed-time" and "breakfast at 7 in the morning."

P. S.—1 o'clock A.M. Since writing the above, I have been luxuriating for half an hour in dream land, undisturbed by the moanings of the billows, or the "taking down the fiddle and the bow" when suddenly aroused by the vision of a boat upset in a squall. I find that the dancers are still hard at it and "the Lancers" are likely to be the order of the balance of the night, and If I don't stop my ears at once and me love to old Morpheus again, while he is in the humor for it, I may lose my lawful rest, go to town with red eyes, and be mistaken for a "fast lady." So, good night and pleasant dreams to you. Rosamond.

Charleston's Mosquito Fleet

T HEY WERE AMONG THE BEST watermen in Charleston's maritime history. Their small boats were a familiar and beloved sight as they sailed out each morning and returned each afternoon with their catch. From the 1860s until the 1950s, the several hundred black fishermen who worked the sailing boats of the mosquito fleet formed the core of Charleston's seafood industry. They fished the creeks, rivers, harbor and, weather permitting, the offshore banks. They would often go as far out as thirty miles to catch porgy, bass, whiting and, if lucky, a "jack fish."

"One by one they shoved off, and lay in the stream while they adjusted their spritsails and rigged their full jibs abeam, like spinnakers, for the free run to the sea," wrote Dubose Heyward, describing Charleston's mosquito fleet in his celebrated novel, *Porgy*. "The vessels were similar in design, the larger ones attaining a length of thirty-five feet. They were very narrow and low in the waist, with high, keen bows, and pointed stern. The hulls were round-bottomed, and had beautiful running lines, the fishermen, who were also the designers and builders, taking great pride in the speed and style of their respective craft. The boats were all open from stem to stern, and were equipped with tholepins for rowing, an expedient to which men resorted only in dire emergency."

In truth, the boats of the mosquito fleet were a motley collection—a hodgepodge of previously used dories, patched-up ship's launches, old lifeboats, hand-hewn bateaux—whatever a clever captain could appropriate or build. Leftovers from the day of sail, they were powered by a mainsail and jib, with a sprit rig designed to be easily dismantled and stowed in the boat while fishing. Manning the oars was only a necessity if the wind failed.

They carried no navigational aids of any kind—not a chart or a compass. They weren't needed. The skippers had an instinctive dead reckoning that even the harbor pilots regarded as "uncanny," and knew their position even when they were out of sight of land.

A reporter for the *News & Courier* wrote a particularly beautiful and apposite article on the mosquito fleet that appeared in the June 15, 1911 edition.

Fishing on the Ocean with the Mosquito Fleet. A Trip to the Fishing Banks Outside the Bar in a Thirty-Foot Open Boat—Queer Ways of the Negro Fishermen. Their Wonderful Keenness of Sight.

Twenty-five miles out at sea in boats, the largest of which is only thirty-two feet in length, each of which is equipped with a mainsail and a jib and manned by a crew of from two to seven men. This would appear to be, and in reality is, one of the most dangerous and exciting methods of fishing on the Atlantic coast. And yet it is and for an unknown number of years has been the method of the fisherman of the mosquito fleet, that collection of minute craft which is as much a part of Charleston as is the water front itself.

It was in the hope of getting some information about the little boats that I strolled down to the head of the wharf, which is the permanent rendezvous of the fleet, one afternoon of last week. It was half-past 3 o'clock and the little boats were just reaching home. What a beautiful sight they presented as they raced up the river in the face of a rather stiff breeze. The boats were close together and it seemed that they would all pull up at the wharf at the same moment. However, the thirty-footers began gradually to nose ahead of the rest, and at last they arrived strung out for a distance of two or three hundred yards.

After the men had disposed of their catches and arranged to go out on the street with whatever they could not sell to the fish house, I entered into conversation with a group who were lounging on the head of the wharf. Finding out that I wished to learn something of their methods of fishing, one of the older men suggested that I make a trip with them some day and see the thing at first hand, a suggestion which I was very eager to accept.

The day arranged for the trip arrived and I was down at the wharf shortly after 6 o'clock. I was to go out in the Dart, the largest and finest boat of the fleet, thirty-two feet on the keel and nearly six feet across at the greatest beam. It took the men nearly an hour to get ready for the trip. A great deal of time being wasted in arguments between the skippers of the boats and the men who wished to go along with them.

Forming a Crew It seemed that all the skippers were afraid of being short-handed . . . [yet] scarcely a man asked permission to go along without being at first rebuffed. In the Dart, the skipper was a young Negro called "Boysey." After about three of the men who fish regularly in the Dart had already got into the boat, several others straggled up and began to ask permission to go out in the Dart. Now the Dart can scarcely go to sea without a crew of five and she generally takes seven or eight. But although there were only four men in the boat at the time, including the skipper, a conversation something like this occurred between "Boysey" and almost every one of these applicants:

"Lemme go out with you to-day Boysey," came from an applicant.

"Why ain't you come when I first tell you can?" This from the skipper.

"I ain't had no bait then. Had to go up the street to borrow the money."

"That ain't my fault."

And right here some one from within the Dart would pipe up with: "We ain't want you in yuh no way, Bally."

After a bit more of this, the applicant would simply step down into the Dart and no one either attempted to stop him or seemed in the least surprised at his presumption.

This went on until there were seven men in the boat besides myself and then it was "Up sails and away," and even as the mainsail was being hoisted, one straggler ran down to the head of the wharf, which we were then rounding, and begged to be taken in. But "Boysey" was obdurate. "We done fill up," and the poor fisherman who was left had no resource excepting to go "shellin'" or fishing from a wharf, for none seemed to be enterprising enough to beg passage from another boat after being turned away from one, and, besides, the Dart was one of the last boats to get away.

Fishing Boats Swift Sailors Although we were among the last to get away, we were not long in overtaking the other boats of the fleet, some of which had as much of a quarter of an hour's start on us. The Dart fairly skimmed the waves and was well in the lead by the time Fort Sumter was passed. She held this lead for a time, but gradually the Maud, a boat which, though not as well constructed, is faster than the Dart, forged to the front and, heading in toward the shore for a large part of the trip out, gained greatly on the Dart, the crew of the latter boat not taking any pains to keep to windward.

Meanwhile, the men in the Dart were engaged in preparing their bait. For bait each had bought two large mullets. These mullets they cut into minute pieces, being very careful not to lose the least bit of meat on the fish. "One o' dem same pieces might catch a jack fish," remarked one. Shark meat is occasionally used for bait, but, as one of the men told me, "mullet got more oil 'n shark." Shrimp also makes up a large part of the bait, since "porgies love shrimp."

While the men were cutting up their bait I asked one of them where the Dart was going that morning. "We got eight men in the boat," he answered. "Tha's too big a crew to go to the whitin' banks, so we goin' out in the deep water, right out to the Gulf." It may be that he meant by this the Gulf Stream, although that body of water does not flow within forty miles of this city.

Right about this time the almost supernatural seamanship of these men was demonstrated. The Dart had passed Morris Island and was well out over the bar. The men began to talk about "that hill over yonder," and "that thar' low spot." I asked them how they remembered the exact positions of these shallows for so many miles outside of the harbor and the skipper replied that he could fish within fifty yards of the same spot every day if he wished to do so. These men, of course, have no instruments for determining their exact location. They use nothing at all but a mariner's compass. It is easily understandable that they should know every inch of the waters to the harbor of the city, but it is nothing short of miraculous that they should have such a knowledge of the waters for fifteen miles outside the bar as to be able to tell from memory when they are in the spot where they fished on the preceding day.

Marvelous Eyesight *To their expert knowledge of the ocean paths is added a keenness of sight, which is a very nearly as marvelous. At one time, just a short while before we reached the grounds, I was given an exhibition of this wonderful eyesight. The Maud was a long distance ahead of us; so far, in fact, that I could see nothing of her outline and to me she appeared only as a dim mass of very small dimension. The skipper of the Dart remarked suddenly that the Maud was about to cast anchor. I asked him how he was able to tell.*

Said he, "Why, ain't you see that man standin' up in her bow soundin'?" More than this, he mentioned the man's name to one of the other men in the Dart, and said that he had not known that the fellow was going out that day. Their eye sight is as intelligent as it is keen, and this was demonstrated on our homeward trip when the skipper saw a squall heading when the sky appeared cloudless, and I strained my eyes in vain to note any change in the atmosphere.

Very soon after this, the Dart also began to take soundings. She was at the first sounding in 7 ½ fathoms. This was not deep enough and the skipper decided to continue the soundings until we had reached at least eight fathoms. At one place the line marked nine fathoms, but here the wind was unfavorable and we moved on about 500 yards further, and finally anchored at a little before 11 o'clock. At that time the Dart was about 26 miles from shore. Not a thing was visible excepting the sea and the sky, and it was only after we had been out about half an hour that another boat drew close enough to us to be seen.

As soon as the sails had been furled and the anchor cast, a great change came over the fishermen. On the trip out, they had been very merry and had been loud in the jokes and laughter. A topic, which had interested them very much, had been the meeting of a lodge, which was to take place that night. One man declared he'd rather miss a meal than miss that meeting. He said, "He sure could give dem fellows de debbil," referring to the novitiates. Another topic, which occupied a great part of their thoughts and speech on the way out, was the relative excellence of certain brands of liquor. Each man proclaimed the glories of his favorite "label" in almost epic flights.

And, in this way, the laughter and merriment had gone on. But now, as soon as the lines were cast over the sides of the boat, all this was hushed. It was not that they were silent through fear of frightening the fish away, or for any reason of this sort. As a matter of fact, they were not silent at all, talking now and then very freely when anything had to be said. It was only because they had no longer interest in anything but their fishing. No songs were sung, no loud laughter now rang out over the water. These men were fishing for blood, and were engaged in a business in which concentration is a very important factor.

Six Fish on a Line *One who has seen only trout fishing with its delicate manipulations of line and bait, or has sat on a wharf for hours on and waiting for "bites," can little appreciate this deep-sea fishing. Each of the men had a line on which were about twelve hooks. A man would cast his line into the water, pull on it once or twice to see if the weight was there, and then pull in. It was a poor haul on which the line did not bring up five or six fish. Rarely did a fisherman allow his line to remain in the water more than two or three minutes. There was no playing with the fish, for none was needed. It was throw out and pull in, with a string of fish for every haul.*

The spot where we had first anchored grew barren of fish very rapidly, and it was 'out oars and get along.' We proceeded in this fashion: I was put at the tiller, because little steering was required. Four men took the oars and pulled in a leisurely manner. Still another man held the 'plum line' and sounded. While the skipper and the eighth man were engaged in "feeling." This last was the most important, since the duty of these two men was to trail their lines in the water and to give notice to the rest when they felt bites of sufficient number to warrant stopping. We proceeded in this way for a few hundred yards, heading south, southeast.

The spot at which the Dart stopped proved to be much more productive of fish than that which she had left. It was shortly after we had arrived here that the skipper caught a jack fish. This was the occasion of joy on his part, and he held the fish up to the admiring and envious gaze of his comrades. A jack fish sometimes brings twenty-five cents in the open market, and this is a great sum in comparison to that received for most of the other fish caught. . . .

After a while the men seemed to grow dissatisfied with the location, and we move down still further. This was our last stopping place.

Shortly after we had arrived here, the skipper gave the word and the boat was started "home-side." It was then about 1 o'clock. In two hours of fishing the seven men had landed over one hundred strings of fish. One man got twenty-five and another twenty-two. A third was unfortunate enough to catch only eight strings.

A Squall *On the way in the men were engaged in stringing their fish. This they did very rapidly and skillfully. The boat fairly flew over the waves and at times was certainly making 15 miles an hour. As she rounded Fort Sumter, the Dart encountered the beginning of a light squall* and if she had raced before her speed now became so great that it seemed as if the impact with the water would break her to pieces. The Dart overtook every other boat on the way in and was nearly 100 yards in the lead when the fleet neared the wharf. In a few minutes she had tied up and the men went off to reap the profits of their day's labor.

As may be supposed, casualties are frequent in this little fleet with its dangerous methods of fishing. The accidents occur mostly in the fall of the year when the weather is so treacherous. Seven years ago three boats containing fifteen men went to the bottom of the sea. Eleven lost their lives in a squall four years ago. Only last fall five men were drowned on one trip.

Yet these men risk their lives day after day, knowing that if a squall of any consequence arises while they are at sea it is very improbable that they will ever return alive. And what, it may be asked, is the guerdon of this perilous occupation? It is exceedingly small, considering the dangers and risks and the average catch of a fisherman will net him about one dollar. On some days a man will catch only enough to cover the expenses of bait and other requisites. The men realize the danger they run, yet there are always enough men to take the places of those what are drowned, and it is probable that the mosquito fleet will continue to exist for as many years in the future as it has existed in the past.

Two weeks after the article above appeared, the following ran in the June 30, 1911 *News & Courier:*

FISHING BOAT LOST AT SEA . . . Skipper and One Member of the Crew of the Uncle Sam Battle for Hours with the Waves, Bearing Drowned Comrade's Body Between them. Survivors Gain Jetties Rescued by Dredge.

Another death was added to the long list of tragedies which mark the history of the mosquito fleet, when the little boat, Uncle Sam, manned by three Negro fishermen, went to the bottom of the sea on Wednesday afternoon, causing the death of one man, Sonny Washington. Cornelius Coaxum, the Captain, and Marcus Brennan, were both saved after a swim, which, they estimate, was three and one-half miles in length, bearing between them the body of their dead comrade. . . .

The skipper of the boat is a quiet Negro, 34 years of age. He appeared to be overwhelmed by the accident which had befallen him and his friends, although it was evidently not wholly unexpected by him. These fishermen, who go to sea in frail shells of boats, almost expect at any moment to be caught by some trick of tide or wind and be dragged to watery graves. Coaxum's father had been drowned in a squall, and so Coaxum, the skipper, was not easily surprised at any tragedy of the deep. He told the story of the drowning about as follows:

Skipper Describes Mishap "It was about 1 o'clock and we were on our way home from the whiting banks, where we had done a good day's work. It was when we were about three and a half miles from the Jetties that the trouble started. It was Sonny Washington's fault. Being captain of the boat, I had given him orders to tend the sail as I thought was right, but he did not think that way, and the first thing I know the Uncle Sam was on top of two seas at once.

"With her bow and her stern both on the crest of waves, I knew she was in a dangerous place. I did not have time to think much, though, because as soon as the bow was cleared the stern rose so that the rudder became unmanageable. Before I knew it the boat had taken a somersault and the three of us were in the water."

In the Water Three and a Half Hours. "It was a little after 1 o'clock. We were in the water until half-past 5 o'clock, or about three and a half hours. I don't know whether Washington could swim or not. Anyway, he did not try to help himself at all, and he lay on his back and sucked in water until he was drowned. Brennan and I were on each side of him when he went under for the last time. We couldn't keep him above water, but we caught him and held him between us. We could see that he was dead already.

"We swam in towards the Jetties with the body between us. A lot of times I thought I couldn't go on any more, but I knew that if I could only get to the Jetties I would be all right. Brennan, from what I could see, was all right the whole way. He is a fine swimmer. We got to the Jetties, three and a half miles, in three and one-half hours. There we lay for about half an hour."

Rescued by the Sumter "The sandsucker, Sumter, found us on the rocks on her way into port. She picked us up and we were given the finest treatment. They gave us something to eat and let us dry and all and I won't forget what they did for me."

When asked what became of the boat, Coaxum said: "I saw her go down and I was glad to see it after what happened. It was the first thing that ever happened to the boat. I was never in any kind of thing like that before and I have been fishing for seventeen years. My father was drowned in the mosquito fleet in a squall ten years ago."

Other Fisherman Not Dismayed This was the first accident of the year in the mosquito fleet. It did not put any damper on the spirits of the other fisherman of the fleet, however. It would require more than the loss of one boat and one man to do that. One of the old men in the fleet remarked yesterday that the whole thing was nothing but 'poor sailing.'

The early summer is not the usual season for casualties in the fleet. It is when the hurricane and squalls sweep suddenly up the coast and catch the men in the midst of their fishing that the real tragedies are enacted. Fifteen men were lost several years ago in one squall. But the daring Negro continues to throw out his mainsail and jib and take his chances twenty miles at sea in a twenty-foot boat in which many people would fear to make a harbor trip.

Hurricane Gracie took the last remaining boats of the mosquito fleet in 1959. Yet these intrepid little sailboats were once a part of the pulse of the old city, the Charleston of yesteryear. Theirs was a time when life was slower; when fish were sold with a song. When

Charleston was a sleepy holdover of the nineteenth century and the fish that the mosquito fleet brought in were sold door-to-door by vendors with wooden pushcarts. The "fish man" would sing loudly about his catch as he slowly pushed his cart down the narrow Charleston streets. "FUSH!!! FRESH FUSH!" the singer would cry. "Oh, de porgy walk, and de porgy talk, De porgy eat with a knife and fork! PORGY! PORGY! FRE-ESH FUSH!"

The New Brighton Hotel

I T WAS, IN A WORD, majestic—a truly grand hotel, three stories tall with turrets and towers and 112 rooms. Completed in June 1884, the New Brighton Hotel was the gem in the setting of the central part of Sullivan's Island called "Atlanticville," located on the front beach at about Station 22 in an area given the alluring name of "Ocean Park." Built by Mr. J.F. Burnham, a "Northern gentleman of means," the New Brighton was to herald a new age of hospitality on the island. Shaped in the form of a large "I," it faced the beach with a spacious, 120- by 40-foot veranda. The center held a long dining hall and, facing the street (then called "Beach Avenue"), was a casino and music hall. Surrounding the main hotel were guest cottages and other outbuildings, including a complete water works, which provided the hotel with hot and cold running water. On the beach were two bathing houses, one for men, the other for ladies. It boasted the most modern conveniences and was accessible from town by ferry and by the then-new Middle Street Railroad. It was the ultimate resort. You couldn't find better outside of Atlantic City.

An article in the March 17, 1884 *News & Courier* touting the New Brighton is excerpted here (and amended for clarity). It provides us with a rare and wonderful look at Sullivan's Island's glory days of the late 1800s.

The advantages of Sullivan's Island as a summer resort are pretty well known all over the South. With its broad beach, affording a clean drive of over three miles, its bracing salt sea breezes, its contiguity to the city . . . it offers attractions for those who would escape from the heat of the summer such as are to be found at very few watering places in the South. While the residents of Charleston . . . have not hesitated to avail themselves of these advantages, very little in the way of attracting visitors from abroad has heretofore been done. The want of proper hotel accommodations has been the most serious drawback . . . but . . . yesterday the Stars and Stripes and the Palmetto flag were floating on the breeze from the flagstaff over the tower of the New Brighton Hotel at Ocean Park, indicating the substantial completion of the new house and the dawn of a new era for our suburb on the sea.

The New Brighton is built on the front beach, about 500 yards to the east end and south of Centennial Hall and the present terminus of the Middle Street Railway track. It is a handsome and imposing structure, stands over nine feet above high water level, and faces the sea . . . built upon brick pillars, which rest upon a solid concrete foundation. The main building has a front of 120 feet and is three stories high, with a Mansard roof and dormer windows. The brick pillars upon which the structure rests are six feet square at the base and rise seven feet. . . . Through these strong iron rods are run beneath the concrete foundation and are clamped to the bottom of huge timbers, which form the sills, and to the joists under the flooring. Iron trusses run through the building from the foundation to the roof and secure the structure, making it as strong as human ingenuity can make it. . . . A spacious piazza 15 feet wide extends the entire length of the building, the roof of the piazza projecting from the top of the second floor. Adjustable blinds will shut out the glare. The French windows on the second floor, some ten in number, open upon small balconies, one to each room, which will give the occupants of the rooms the opportunity of enjoying the sea breezes without the necessity of joining the throng on the general promenade. On the first floor are the office, the reading room, ladies' parlor, reception room, nursery, and baggage-room. A branch of the Middle Street Railway track will run directly to the doors of the hotel and will land passengers on the spot. Three new cars . . . will run over the Middle Street Railway exclusively for the guests of the house and in close connection with the boats from the ferry company. Broad hallways run through the building in every direction, ensuring the most thorough ventilation and the circulation of the sea breeze. The sleeping rooms, of which there are 112, will be fitted up in the most thorough and comfortable manner, and the wainscoting and finishings of the interior will be handsome and appropriate.

The central part of the "I" of the hotel was the dining room, which measured 40 by 90 feet, with 15-foot high ceilings, lighted and ventilated by eighteen windows. The walls and ceiling were paneled and it was "thoroughly equipped. Under the dining room, and extending about half its length, is a monster cistern, with a capacity of 65,000 gallons. The water will be forced up from this to a tank on a tower situated near the eastern end of the building, whence it will be distributed through the house by a complete system of water pipes. Adjoining the cistern under the dining room is a cellar 40 by 45 feet, built of solid brick and Portland cement, and to be used for the storing of provisions, wines, etc." Given the topography of the island, one wonders how they dealt with the danger of hitting water while constructing this cistern and basement. It must have been quite an engineering feat.

The casino end of the building faced the street and mirrored the front beach end. It included billiard rooms, poolrooms and saloons, with the upper stories reserved for sleeping quarters. "The first floor will be devoted to amusements. It will consist of a hall capable of seating 500 or more persons and provided with a stage, scenery, etc. It is proposed during the summer to give a series of musical and dramatic entertainments, and arrangements will be made which will enable the city people to run over to the Island, attend a concert or ball, or whatever is in progress, and return to the city for about the same amount as is charged for admission to the Academy of Music."

The season opened with a two-week engagement of one of the most celebrated bands in the nation, the Reaves American Band and Orchestra. "During their engagement, which has been effected at a cost of $1,800 per week, excluding travelling expenses and board, two concerts will be given daily at the New Brighton Casino—an afternoon concert by the military band [from Fort Moultrie] and instrumental concert at night by the orchestra. They will be followed by the famous Vienna female orchestra, whose admirable concerts at the Atlantic Gardens in New York have probably been heard by many Charlestonians."

Surrounding the hotel were servants' quarters and a kitchen, "fitted up with one of the best ranges from Bramhall & Dean, with portable brick ovens and large hot-water tanks and boilers." Also there were "semi-detached" cottages, each containing eight to ten rooms, connected to the hotel office by means of "electric bells, speaking tubes, etc., and, like the rooms in the hotel proper . . . handsomely furnished with all the latest and most improved conveniences."

On the beach itself were two bathing houses, which stood "near the high water mark on the beach . . . divided into dressing rooms neatly and comfortably furnished, [with] bathing suits provided, and in each house . . . an office in which a safe will be kept for the deposit of the valuables of the bathers. A wooden plankway will take the bather directly to the surf and enable him to reach his dressing-room without wading through the sand. Both houses will be supplied with bath-tubs and fresh water by a complete system of water-works connected with the main system. They will also be lighted with gas."

The building's sturdy construction enabled it to withstand several Hugo-sized hurricanes in the late 1800s and early 1900s. Sadly, a fire eventually destroyed it. But in its day, the

New Brighton was majestic, "a splendid modern edifice, with all the comforts and conveniences required by modern civilization, upon an historic and attractive spot, with balmy breezes and mild temperatures."

Isle of Palms:
That Unknown Country

Today, with the upscale Wild Dunes area and its lavish beach-front homes, it is difficult to imagine the island as it was originally—a long, uninhabited strip of sand and interior jungle. There are many islanders who bemoan the development (or over-development) that has taken place on the island in recent years. Yet Isle of Palms has developed into *exactly* what it was originally intended to become. From the outset, the plans were to take this oceanfront island and transform it into a nationally recognized residential resort.

Isle of Palms was the brainchild of wealthy Charlestonian, Dr. Joseph Lawrence, who foresaw creating a majestic, Atlantic City-style resort out of the barrier island wilderness that would attract people from all over the country. He also saw the island eventually becoming a year-round residential community. His was an early version of "if you build it, they will come," and he was right.

It took a tremendous amount of work and money. There was nothing on the island, not even a bridge, so Lawrence's "Long Island Improvement Company" not only faced the job of erecting a resort hotel and pavilion, they had to create roads, bridges, a new ferry boat operation and, last but not least, establish and lay the tracks for a trolley line. In July 1898, the island formerly known as Long Island officially opened as "Isle of Palms" and was an immediate success.

"A GREAT EVENT FOR THE CITY," blared *Courier* front-page headlines on July 26, 1898. "THE SEASHORE ROAD FORMALLY OPENED YESTERDAY. When the Commodore Perry left the new dock of the Charleston & Seashore Railway Company at 3 o'clock yesterday afternoon her spacious deck was crowded with people, all anxious to be among the first to visit that, as yet, unknown country, stretching vaguely behind the familiar shores of Mount Pleasant and Sullivan's Island. The Sappho, her deck also crowded with people, and the Pocosin, not so well patronized, steamed out of their docks just a moment before."

Literally thousands of people took the fifteen-minute ferry ride from the city to Mount Pleasant where the crowds then boarded Dr. Lawrence's new trolley cars. "The inhabitants of the green little city of Mount Pleasant turned out in a body . . . to give the trolley a genial greeting as it sped on its way . . . many were the prophecies of the great things to come to Mount Pleasant through the trolley line . . . of which owe so much to the public spirit and enterprise of Dr. Lawrence."

The trolley then crossed Dr. Lawrence's newly built trestle bridge (which we know today as the Old Bridge) to Sullivan's Island. "On the trestles and bridges," wrote the *Courier*, "very fast time was made. Indeed, the most nervous old lady in Charleston will have no cause to feel timid in crossing these trestles, which are built in the most careful and substantial manner." Even today, at the end of the Old Bridge you can see the iron remains of the old trolley track.

From here, the trolley journeyed the length of Sullivan's Island, passing Fort Moultrie and the new mortar battery, the "hill" fort in the center of that island.

The boys in blue all welcomed the trolley with hurrahs and cap-waving. By and by the closed and deserted Atlantic Beach Hotel [at Station 22], which every one wishes open, was passed. About a mile and a half beyond . . . is the bridge over Breach Inlet, which, including its approaches, is 1,200 feet long. This bridge over Breach Inlet is considered quite an engineering feat, as many people thought it was not possible to bridge the inlet. But it has been done and successfully done, for though the tide was rushing through the inlet at a tremendous pace, those who were in the car felt as though they were riding on solid ground, and were only reminded of the fact that they were in reality crossing the water by looking out upon the rippling waves on either side of the car.

Finally, the *Courier* continued, the passengers reached Isle of Palms.

Upon entering the (to most of the passengers) unknown region of the Isle of Palms—formerly called Long Island, but now variously designated "Pam" or "Parm" Island, according to whether the speaker is in the habit of going North in the summer or not—this region is found to be very much elevated above the sea. It is practically clear of trees, with the exception of low shrubbery, for about a mile and a half. It is the intention of the Long Island Improvement Company to devote this end of the island to the summer residences, and as soon as the hills can be leveled and the lots laid out, they will be placed upon the market. At the end of this "sand hill" portion of the island is the station. With the exception of the beach and a row of sand hills just behind the beach, this portion is covered with a beautiful growth of palmettoes, which picturesque trees, growing in great profusion, have given their name to the island. Among them are spreading live oaks, cedars all covered at this season with their tiny bluish berries, and many other evergreens, which will make the Isle of Palms as pleasant to the eye in winter as it is now in the summer time. This is the part of the island which is to be given up to winter residences. It will be divided up into villa sites of several acres each, and will be laid out with beautiful roads and drives.

Another important part of Dr. Lawrence's vision was providing a place at the beach that day-trippers could enjoy. "These accommodations . . . will be a great convenience and comfort to the patrons of the road," noted the Courier. "Formerly on Sullivan's Island, even when the hotel was open, people who went to the Island for only a day's outing felt a delicacy about sitting on the hotel piazza, or otherwise making use of it unless they were guests of the house, and most people who spend a day on the Island even now have to borrow a friend's house, or bake in the sun all day, if they are no so fortunate as to have friends living on the Island. The Seashore Railway has changed all this. For this immense pavilion is the property of the road, and those people who pay their fare to Long Island will have a perfect right to sit in the pavilion, or on the verandah chairs on the broad piazza which surrounds it."

In August 1898, the News & Courier predicted, "the seaside re-sort will bring thousands of visitors this way every year who would not have come otherwise." Throughout this past century, there have been times when Isle of Palms was close to the attainment of Dr. Lawrence's original vision. Today, it is a full reality.

The Islands During World War II

SOLDIERS BEGIN FIRING. Danger Zones Announced at Fort Moultrie.

Preliminary firing began yesterday at Fort Moultrie with the rifle, pistol and machine gun, but results will not be available until the latter part of the week.

Danger zones which have been announced for rifle practice follow:

Marshall reservation and its beaches, south of highway 703, and area southeast thereof between a line from danger flag on 65 degrees magnetic azimuth and line from southwest corner of Marshall reservation on 145 degrees azimuth, extending seaward 6,600 yards. Office in charge of the range is Major Thomas J. Chrisman, commanding officer, Second battalion, Eighth infantry.

For the pistol and machine gun firing, the danger zone will be as follows:

Sector included between the lines on magnetic azimuth 135 and 220 degrees from radio tower at old Fort Moultrie, extending seaward as far as north edge of main channel, including the beaches.

Dates for firing are from June 26, yesterday, until July 29. Time for practice each day is from 7 a.m. until 7 p.m. for the rifle, and 7 a.m. until 4:30 p.m for machine gun and pistols. All persons are asked to observe the danger zones.

—From the June 27, 1939, News & Courier.

I've been told that when there was practice firing of the massive guns that lined the island during World War II, the sound was so loud and reverberations so strong that window glass shattered and plates and glassware fell from kitchen cabinets in broken heaps. I think that, eventually, the practice firing was mollified somewhat to prevent this island-wide breakage. Yet the story tells volumes of how seriously Sullivan's Island was fortified during World War II.

One who remembered the island during the war was former Sullivan's Island mayor and font of island knowledge—the dearly departed and sorely-missed Melvin Anderegg. One day several years ago he called to tell me that erosion on the beach around Stations 29 and 30 had unearthed the circular outline of one of the beachfront batteries erected during the war. For those not familiar with the island, this is the northernmost end of the island at Breach Inlet. During World War II, this end of the island was called Marshall Reservation and was literally covered with military barracks, support buildings and a variety of armed batteries.

Melvin Anderegg was a boy on the island during World War II and it only took slight coaxing on my part to get him to describe the island during the war. "The entire beachfront was dotted with batteries," he explained, "and these were supported by other batteries built on the high ridge at the back of the island, where Gold Bug Avenue is now. Around Station 17, in front of the Island Club, they had sand bag emplacements with machine guns. There was a canine corps on Marshall Reservation, at about Station 28 or 29 on Middle Street, and at night the guys patrolled the beaches with dogs, in case any Germans or saboteurs landed.

"The submarine nets came in at Station 19—great big, long, high cables, at least 4 to 6 inches in diameter with big spikes. These ran all the way out to the jetties. There was also a submarine net across the channel opening between the jetties, which was raised and lowered to allow ships to pass. The inland waterway had movable submarine nets, and you can still see the remains of a permanent one that had been placed across the opening of Conch Creek.

"Interestingly," he continued, chuckling, "fish often got trapped on the Charleston side of the nets at Station 19 off the front beach. Sharks, in fact. People got worried because the sharks, being all penned in, had become aggressive. We boys used to dive off the submarine nets at Station 19. It was like walking a tightrope."

"Didn't you worry about the sharks?" I asked.

Laughing, he said, "Well, just a little."

Anderegg described how there were beachfront batteries on all the islands north of the island, up to Bull's Island. "A communications cable ran all the way from Sullivan's Island to Bull's," he said. "It went under Breach Inlet, all the way across Isle of Palms, under that inlet, across Dewees and Capers and, finally, linked up with the batteries on Bull's Island."

The central part of this cable was made of copper wire, and Anderegg explained how, after the war, island residents tried all sorts of creative ways to salvage parts of the cable. Buried from three to four feet underground, around the central core of copper wires was a lead sheeting, coated with a burlap sheathing and then covered with tar to make it waterproof. Around all this was stranded steel cable to keep it from being cut by a dragging anchor. It was a job to pull the cable up, but it brought good money at the salvage yard.

"Everybody had a little secret place where they worked at pulling up the cable," he said. "They'd hide the end of the cable under sea grass or anything else handy, so that nobody would notice. Everybody had their own method. Some tied big floating logs to the cable, hoping that the ebb and flow of the tide, banging the cable up and down, would shake it loose. Others would dig up one end of the cable, get a barrel, bend the cable over the barrel and then take their automobile (you could drive on the beach then), and hook onto the cable that way. It was tough work, and even if you got twenty or thirty feet of cable, then you had to hacksaw through it."

How much was thirty feet of cable worth at the salvage yard? "Oh, $30 or so." he said. "But then, at that time, a good salary was $70 a month. I remember when the soldiers at the fort, who'd been living on $18, got a raise to $21. They thought they'd hit a gold mine."

Today, with Marshall Reservation now studded with exquisite houses and manicured lawns, it is hard to imagine the extent of military history here. Even the huge hill batteries, erected in 1943, have been transformed into private homes. Such residences have sometimes hidden advantages. Bob Curd, who has also passed on to the great hill fort in the sky, lived in the hill battery named "Battery Marshall" during the time that Hurricane Hugo slammed the island with such ferocity. Almost every house on the island suffered extensive damage except for Curd's. But then, his home was covered with who-knows-how-many feet of concrete topped with tons of earth.

Curd loved to tell the story of being called by a not-so-honest roofer from Summerville some weeks after the storm. Curd listened patiently while the man explained how, while he had been driving through the island, he had noticed that Curd's roof was in such bad shape that it would need to be entirely replaced. He also added that he'd do the job at a rock-bottom price.

"Really?" answered Curd, no doubt stifling an urge to laugh out loud. "Then you come on by in the morning and tell me how much it will cost." The next morning, with his cup of coffee in hand, Curd stood outside the back door of his massive hill fort and waited for the roofer to arrive. Sure enough, the roofer drove up, took one look at the grassy mound that formed the so-called "roof" of Bob's house, saw Bob standing there with what can only be described as a roofer-eating grin, and fled without saying a word.

Big Blows

G ET OUT THE FLASHLIGHT BATTERIES, light the candles and pull the
Sterno out from the back of the closet. Another hurricane season
looms on the horizon. To soothe your nerves I thought I might pass
along a few first-hand narratives about some of the big blows that have
hit Charleston in the past.

On September 15, 1752, one of the most catastrophic storms ever
to hit Charleston roared in. This Hugo-sized storm began about four
in the morning and raged until nine, when, according to the *South Carolina Gazette,*

*The FLOOD came in like a bore, filling the harbor in a few minutes. Before 11 o'clock, all the
vessels in the harbor were on shore, except the Hornet man-of-war which rode it out by cutting away
her main-mast; all the wharves and bridges were ruined, and every house, store, &c, upon them
beaten down, and carried way (with all the goods, &c. therein.) The town was likewise overflowed,
the tide or sea having rose upwards of Ten feet above the high-water mark at spring-tides, and nothing was now to be seen but ruins of houses, canows, wrecks of pettiaugers and boats, masts, yards,
incredible quantities of all sorts of timber, barrels, staves, shingles, household and other goods,
floating and driving, with great violence, thro' the streets, and round about the town.*
*The inhabitants, finding themselves in the midst of a tempestuous sea, the wind still continuing,
the tide (according to its common course) being expected to flow 'till after one o'clock, and many of*

the people already being up to their necks in water in their houses; began now to think of nothing but certain death: they were soon delivered from their apprehensions for, about 10 minutes after 11 o'clock, the wind veered to the E.S.E. and S.W. very quick…the waters fell about 5 feet in the space of 10 minutes, without which unexpected and sudden fall, every house and inhabitant in them, must, in all probability, have perished.

As it was many drowned. The pesthouse on Sullivan's Island was swept away. One ship with a cargo of Palatines was driven from her anchorage into the marsh near to James Island where, by continuing rolling the passengers were tumbled from side to side. About twenty of them, by bruises and other injuries lost their lives.

The pest house had fifteen people inside when it was swept off Sullivan's Island. It apparently found land again somewhere near Hobcaw Point. Five people survived that trip, which must have been one heck of a Nantucket sleigh ride.

The Great Gale of 1804 came in on September 11, when "A STORM which it is said has not been equaled within the memory of any citizen of Charleston, commenced on Friday evening last," wrote the *News & Courier* as soon as they were able to publish. "Great apprehensions were entertained for the safety of the families on Sullivan's Island. . . 15-20 houses were undermined by the water and washed away. If the water had continued to rise for half an hour longer, scarcely a house would have escaped, and many people would have perished."

Off Cape Romain, several vessels were caught in the midst of this powerful hurricane. Three were cast ashore on Bull's Island. The schooner *Favourite*, from Baltimore, was not so fortunate. It sank almost immediately after the storm hit. "There were on board at the time, Captain Culley, his mate, and three passengers," reported the *Courier* a week later. "Mr. and Mrs. Groves [and] a Mr. Stewart . . . and a negro fellow, said to be the property of a Mr. Wescott. Mr. Groves and a seaman by the name of Wallace, caught hold of a hen coop, the other persons on board, it is believed, went down with the vessel. Wallace kept his hold on the coop about four hours, when exhausted, he fell off and drowned. Mr. Groves was then left alone, and remained in this situation until Sunday evening at 6 o'clock (12 hours) when he was fortunately picked up by Captain Smith of the Venus, from New York."

Caroline Gilman was on Sullivan's Island with her children and house servants during this storm. She later wrote, "it . . . rose and rose like some living monster preparing itself for a death-struggle, until the waves lifted the piazza. It was no longer safe, and we looked abroad in desperation, while our voices could scarcely be heard amid the roar of the elements. Moving masses of ruins were seen floating on the white foam; beyond, all was intense darkness."

Knowing the house was no longer safe they attempted to make their way to Fort Moultrie for safety. "It came—the gale rushed with ten thousand voices, thundering on, roaring and raging over bursting waves; we clung to each other still more firmly, but we were parted as easily as gossamer tufts in the south winds of summer." It was not until the next morning that they found each other. Incredibly, all were alive except for one servant, who was never found. The baby, Patsey, was discovered on the beach. "Some fisherman, at the early dawn...perceived one of their boats high on the sand, capsized and resting on some timbers. They raised it, and there lay Patsey, our little cherub, wrapped in her nurse's apron, and sleeping in her arms."

Hurricane of August 27, 1813

THERE IS A LONG-SAID ditty about hurricanes that goes, "June, too soon—July, go by; August, be cautious—September, REMEM-BER!" Late August can bring ferocious storms and one of the worst storms in Charleston's history was the August storm of 1813. It was dramatically described in the *Charleston Courier*, the reporter obviously unafraid to take full poetic license. It was not unusual for nineteenth-century reporters to place added emphasis to articles by capitalizing dramatic or emphatic phrases. He gets his point across:

On Friday night last we experienced one of the most TREMENDOUS GALES of wind that ever was felt on our coast. The HORRORS OF THAT AWFUL NIGHT we shall not attempt to portray; but the particulars of its DESOLATING EFFECTS, so far as they have come to our knowledge, will be given with as much accuracy as the nature of the base admits. TORRENTS OF RAIN accompanied the gale, and the tide, which should have been high before 10 o'clock continued rising until 12, at which time it was about 18 inches higher than in the GREAT GALE OF 1804,

Many families whose dwellings are in low situations were DRIVEN FROM THEIR HOMES through the PELTING OF THE PITILESS STORM to seek shelter among the more fortunate neighbors. Others again, particularly in that part of the city fronting the north and northeast, had the lower rooms of their houses COMPLETELY INUNDATED and were unable to leave them, unless indeed in boats, which was done in some instances. Others were in vain CRYING FOR

ASSISTANCE expecting every moment when the vessels which were THROWN UPON THE WHARVES, to hear them CRUSH THEIR HOUSES and BURY THEM IN THE RUINS. More than half the new bridge over the Ashley River was SWEPT AWAY by the violence of the storm and the GREAT RISE OF WATER must have floated the top from the piers, and the fragments in large bodies DRIFTED DOWN WITH THE TIDE and lodged upon South Bay and elsewhere.

In August 1813, Sullivan's Island was a popular spot. People from Charleston and inland plantations "resorted" to the island each summer, fleeing the city's heat and humidity, but more importantly, escaping the deadly mosquito-borne diseases that plagued town and country. They came for the island's fresh air and "salubrious" climate. Entire families moved to the island in May, sometimes not returning to the city until October and/or the first killing frost. The homes were honest-to-goodness beach houses—nothing fancy, just comfortable, board-and-batten homes with wide porches and plenty of open windows to catch the southerly breeze. Not everyone was impressed with the island's relaxed lifestyle. Edgar Allan Poe described the island's houses as "miserable huts," and in 1817, visitor Francis Hall described island cottages as "miserable wooden tenements." Even so, the houses served their purpose. They provided a place of refuge from disease. Hurricanes, however, were another matter.

When a hurricane hit in those days, it hit without warning. With the onset of rising tides and gale winds, people did their best to batten down, close the shutters on the windows and ride out the storm, but rarely was there enough time to adequately evacuate to higher ground. If the water started rising, people often attempted to reach the newly completed Fort Moultrie. Sometimes they made it. Sometimes they didn't.

The storm of 1813 was one such storm and the island was completely inundated by the tidal surge. Wrote the *Courier* of the destruction on Sullivan's Island: "In the morning THE ISLAND exhibited a MOST MELANCHOLY PICTURE; fragments of houses, furniture, boats, etc. were thrown promiscuously over it, and the BODIES OF NINE PERSONS, four of them females, lay among the ruins, an awful remembrance of THE HORRORS of the night before. . . . It is supposed that as many as FIFTEEN HAVE PERISHED."

Following this storm, the islanders buried the dead, picked up the pieces and rebuilt. After all, hurricanes, like pestilent diseases, were simply part of life in the Carolina Lowcountry—something to be contended with each late summer and fall; something you couldn't do anything about and simply learned to expect.

Thankfully, vaccines have eradicated the deadly epidemics of earlier eras. Hurricanes, however, are still with us. They are forces of nature, which seem to have a mind of their own.

The Great Hurricane of 1911

THE HURRICANE OF AUGUST 27, 1911, was perhaps the worst to hit the coast prior to Hugo in 1989. It came in on Sunday, with little warning while both Sullivan's Island and Isle of Palms were filled with vacationers. The following, much of which is gleaned from newspaper reports, not only tells the story of this great hurricane, but also provides a clear look at life on the islands at that time.

Ah, the summer of 1911! The beautiful Atlantic Beach Hotel was in full swing, offering special weekend rates of $2.00 a day, "from supper Saturday up to and including breakfast Monday." A main feature of the hotel was the hop, or dance, held every Saturday evening at 8 p.m. There was also music on Sunday night by the First Artillery Orchestra. "Come and enjoy the cool breezes at this popular resort with us" touted an advertisement in the News & Courier. "Rates $10 to $18 Per Week. Brown & Jacobs, Lessees."

The new resort called Isle of Palms was barely ten years old and the magnificent Seashore Hotel, owned by James Sotille, was the hottest spot in town. The Seashore also offered special rates as well as a daily fish dinner. "Come and try one for 75 cents," read the ad. "Special Weekend Vacation trips from Dinner Saturday Night until

Monday Morning. One and a half days for $3. B. Dub and Jack H. Clancey, Managers, Hotel and Cafe."

What a carefree time was that summer of 1911. Weekends saw the Consolidated Railway Company ferry boats, the *Lawrence* and *Sappho*, plying the waters from Charleston to Mount Pleasant, literally packed with beach goers. Landing at the Mount Pleasant ferry dock near Alhambra Hall, vacationers then took the trolley over to Sullivan's Island, getting off at whatever "station" they wished, or continuing on across Breach Inlet to Isle of Palms. This was an untroubled time in Charleston—a time when men were decked out in flannel whites and straw boaters; when ladies only entered the water from bathing houses set out on the beach, dressed in an appropriate "bathing costume," a frilly, pantalooned affair in which they were only a bit less fully clothed than in their usual floor-length frocks.

Big news that summer was the sinking of the pontoon, or floating dock, at the Mount Pleasant Ferry Terminal. "More than Two and a Half Thousand People Visit Seashore Resort in Spite of Accident," read the headlines, followed by this rather glib report, so consistent with the relaxed times:

Nothing could stop the inhabitants of Charleston and some hundreds of people from other less favored cities from going to the Isle of Palms yesterday—not even the fact that the big float or pontoon at the Mount Pleasant end of the ferry had become tired of life and committed suicide some little time before the sun rose. The float decided that it had been a float long enough at about 3 o'clock yesterday morning. Accordingly, it sank with a soft gurgle into the waters of the bay, and at present rests quietly on the mud that girds the shores of beautiful Mount Pleasant.

It didn't make any real difference. The crowds were going to the Isle of Palms, float or no float; and the ferry people proved that they could get along very well without the pontoon.

If we think the beaches are crowded now, read on:

Although yesterday's crowd at the Isle of Palms, numbering 2,751 people, was almost exactly 100 people smaller than that of the previous Sunday, little difference could be noted. Excursions from the points around Charleston brought hundreds of visitors and most of them went to the Island.

The dressing rooms in the bath houses were well filled, and the beach was lined with bathers throughout the afternoon and early evening. The facilities for this branch of the Island have been increased and larger crowds can now be handled with greater ease. The surf was rolling splendidly, and the bathers had great sport with the large waves.

The concert, however, was the real feature of the afternoon, the musicians receiving round after round of applause at the completion of each selection. The people were crowded around the band-stand, and showed a thorough appreciation of the music rendered by Metz's Band.

Visitors numbered nearly 3,000 people a weekend on Isle of Palms. Think of it! And only a decade earlier, the island had been all but deserted.

Sunday, August 27, began with a wind and light rains, yet the weather didn't dampen the spirits of Isle of Palms excursionists. So popular was the resort that the Sunday paper had a lavish article about Miss Maud Odell, "the popular South Carolina actress," who was visiting the Seashore Hotel and had nothing but praise to say about the island:

"Look at the magnificent situation, the great turbulent ocean on one side, just throwing tons of ozone into you, and the reposeful beautiful river and those shady green trees on the other. Where else could you find such a combination? I predict that this place will be the Atlantic City of the south in a few years. . . . When all the present plans of improving this already beautiful spot are carried out, believe me, it will be 'good night Palm Beach.' "

In the long run, her predictions about the island came true. In the short run, however, the island was courting disaster. For that very afternoon, while thousands of people on both islands were enjoying the "ozone" from the sea, the wind rose, the sea turned into a broiling cauldron and the elements were unleashed.

"CHARLESTON IN GRIP OF ROARING HURRICANE," read the headlines on the morning of the 28th. "THE WORST SINCE MEMORABLE STORM OF 1893.

Mass of Ruins. What was once the most beautiful seashore resort of the Atlantic coast is now transposed into a mass of debris. The car terminal for the Consolidated Railway, at the entrance of the pavilion, and the car station at the Seashore Hotel, is entirely demolished. . . .

"The News and Courier goes to press this morning in the midst of what may prove to be the most terrific hurricane that has passed over this city since August 4, 1893.

"The storm came unexpected," stated the Courier. "Charlestonians went to bed Saturday night with clear skies above and the stars keeping watch in the heavens. Shortly before midnight clouds

began to cover the eastern portion of the skies and by midnight rain was falling. The barometer ordinarily falls in the nighttime between 10 o'clock and 4 a.m. after which it begins to rise again. Saturday night it fell till 4 a.m., but instead of rising it continued to fall steadily."

There were fifteen hundred Sunday excursionists on Isle of Palms. No one took any note of the elements until the early afternoon, when the storm began "to take up a serious aspect." The first afternoon boat left the island at three o'clock, carrying about 800 people.

"From the mainland many watched with intense interest the passage of the big ferry boat, the Lawrence," reported the Courier. "The wind was blowing 45 miles an hour and the harbor presented a rough sea. . . . The passengers had a rough passage and as soon as the platform of the boat was coupled with the gang plank they made a wild break for terra firma.

"In the rush from the boat a number of women were overcome and several fainted in the press of the crowd. Children screamed out with fright and others with pain, as their toes were trampled on in the wild rush. Three hundred and fifty people still remained on the Island and Superintendent Passalaigue, of the Consolidated, was anxious to get them to the mainland, for he had received word direct from the weather office to exercise the best efforts in getting the crowds off the island. The sea was so rough that Mr. Passalaigue told the master of the boat to use his judgment and not risk the trip unless he felt safe in doing so.

The *Lawrence* made the run back to Mount Pleasant, but no farther. Those remaining on Isle of Palms and Sullivan's Island were stranded.

Notwithstanding the threatening aspect of the weather yesterday afternoon . . . over seventy-five had been in bathing all afternoon. . . . The people . . . expected to take the 4:30 train and to get back to the city about 8 o'clock last night. But when the ferryboat Lawrence started back across the harbor she could not make the trip. The result is that 350 people, nearly all excursionists from out of town who failed to pay sufficient heed to the warnings. . . .

The pavilion on the Isle of Palms would have furnished little protection to anyone in it. Reports made by three arriving in the city at 6 o'clock yesterday afternoon were to the effect that the waves had already reached the pavilion when they left and that the breakers were mounting steadily.

On Sullivan's Island, not only were people housed at the Atlantic Beach Hotel, but also almost all the summer cottages (which now reached all the way up to Station 28) were filled with their usual summer residents. Some 500 people were on the island on the night of the 27th.

"The night was a creepy one, the wind roaring over the city, the ceaseless rattle of slates and tins wrenched from roofs, the crash of chimneys falling into the streets or alleys, the inky blackness, the awe-inspiring thunder of the waves in the harbor as they dashed furiously against the wharves and the sea walls, and worst of all, the uncertainty of it all, were enough to make the stoutest heart quail."

—From the *News & Courier*, Tuesday Morning, August 29, 1911:

SIX DEATHS, PROBABLY $1,000,000 DAMAGE DONE. HURRICANE PASSES AFTER WORKING MUCH INJURY. ISLANDERS BROUGHT TO CITY. SAPPHO AND CYPRESS BRING 500 REFUGEES. No Deaths or Injuries Reported on Sullivan's Island Yesterday—Soldiers at Fort Show Heroism and Assist Terror-stricken Islanders in Every Manner Possible—Damage Estimate Impossible.

Five hundred or more of those who passed through the storm on Sullivan's Island Sunday night were brought to the city yesterday afternoon by the Sappho and Government boat Cypress. Although the storm was one of the severest in the history of the island, there were no deaths or injuries reported. This seems almost impossible, as there are hundreds of cottages destroyed and damaged, and the Consolidated Railway is a mass of debris from Mount Pleasant to the terminal at the Isle of Palms. The reasons perhaps for the safety of the people . . . is due in a large measure to the . . . heroism of the soldiers who patrolled the Island during the night, aiding those in distress and keeping the people posted on the storm. . . . Many of the cottages were blown down but in every instance those who inhabited them had been removed to a point of safety in the Government reservation or the house of some friend. The water on the beach in First Street was very high, in some instances higher than the average man's head and on the back beach it was hard to get from one point to another without assistance. Most of the damage to cottages was on the beach, and the smaller houses in other parts of the Island were destroyed or damaged. The wind reached an enormous velocity on the Island about 2 o'clock yesterday morning, and it was about this time that most of the damage was done. . . .

A young man laughingly told of how he and two companions fought a hundred mile wind in water almost waist deep with three women and a sick man, for nearly half a mile to safety; another told of how the soldiers formed a life line by holding each other's hands and saved a woman and two children just before the cottage was blown down. There are hundreds of instances of this sort. . . .

At one portion of the narrow strip forming Sullivan's Island [later reported as Station 18], the writhing sea lashed its way cross the entire width of the Island, joining forces with the back water, itself by that time changed from placidity to churning fury.

And what of the people at the Seashore Hotel? The following report in the *News & Courier* carries shades of the sinking of the *Titanic*.

"GUESTS MADE MERRY," ran the headline. "MUSIC WHILE STORM RAGED".

'Notwithstanding the fact that one of the most terrible storms which had ever visited this port was raging for many hours, all the guests made merry,' said Mr. Schaefer [a businessman from Atlanta.] 'The staunch Seashore Hotel withstood the storm, except for a portion of the left wing, which was carried away, as were the servants' quarters. It was necessary to nail and brace every door and window in the hotel. The ladies bravely took things as they were, and each and every one in her role proved herself a heroine.

'Miss Dub presided at the piano during the height of the storm, while the misses Mildred and Ethel Guckenhemer, entertained with singing and recitations. Several young gentlemen deserve special mention for their brave efforts in boarding up windows and doors, barring out the terrible wind and storm. Those deserving special mention in doing this effective work are: Mesrs. Edw. C. Stothart, Robt. Magwood, Jas Allan, Jr., and Mr. James Sotill e, the owner of Isle of Palms, who led his little band of brave men through every part of the house making things as secure as possible from the storm.'

The worst damage, however, was to the more heavily occupied Sullivan's Island. "That more houses have been damaged and destroyed on Sullivan's Island than ever before," stated the *Courier*, "is the opinion of Mr. Oscar E. Johnson, who was one of the business men who came to the city yesterday afternoon on the *Sappho*. . . .

Mr. Johnson, who lives on the farthest end of the Island, at Station 26 ½, had an experience Sunday night which he does not care to repeat. There were about a dozen people in the house in which he was staying. At 10 o'clock, when the wind changed, they were driven from the house and forced to make their way through water that was both deep and swift to another. They accomplished this with difficulty, but no sooner had they gotten to the second house than the piazza was blown away and then the roof. The men of the party were compelled to brace the doors to prevent them from being blown down; fearing that if this should happen the house itself would go to pieces.

Many did. That belonging to Messrs. Isaac Ball and Campbell crashed just after they had left it. No one was hurt. Another house fell while a man, a woman and five or six children were on the back steps. All escaped uninjured. Dr. Sprunt's house was among those blown out of position. Mr. Johnson considers it mir aculous that so much damage should have been done to property on Sullivan's Island and yet no one be hurt.

As the week following the hurricane brought more news from outlying areas, the truly ferocious damage of this hurricane was evident.

The death toll kept rising, with seventeen eventually killed. A collapsing house killed a woman in Mount Pleasant; another woman, thinking her house was about to give way, threw her children out the window. Luckily, they survived. An entire family was lost at Wappoo Cut. Two men were crushed to death when the ticket office of the Consolidated Ferry wharf in Mount Pleasant collapsed on them.

In Mount Pleasant, then a sleepy village surrounded by farmland, it was reported by residents that "they believed that the wind blew much harder there than on the mainland. The Town Hall was blown, the Consolidated car shed was unroofed, the ferry ticket office was destroyed, the ferry bridgeway washed away and a number of residences unroofed."

Possibly the worst news came later, when it was discovered that the Lowcountry's entire rice crop was destroyed. The dikes were broken, the fields flooded with salt water; it was the final death knell for rice farming in South Carolina, ending over three hundred years of world-renowned Carolina Golden Rice.

The weeks following the storm are reminiscent of the aftermath of Hugo. Advertisements abounded for roofing tiles, glass, hardware and insurance. Proving that nothing really changes throughout history, there was severe criticism of the Weather Bureau for not giving ample warning of the storm. Still, the prognosis for rebuilding was positive. "HUM OF BUSINESS GOES MERRILY ON," read the headlines, "OPTIMISM KEYNOTE OF COMMENT." One report began, "probably no one will reap as much benefit from the hurricane as the tinners, carpenters, slaters and glaziers. These men will have their hands full of work for many weeks and there is said to be plenty of room in the city for many more men engaged in these occupations." Those who experienced Hugo know this scenario all too well.

The Hurricane of 1911 was followed by a string of lesser storms, one each year until 1916, then there was a break until September 18, 1928, when a fierce hurricane damaged the construction of the Cooper River Bridge and killed five people. The next major hurricane was not until 1940, a severe storm with a 13-foot tidal surge, killing thirty-four people. In 1952, the weather service began naming hurricanes, and on October 15, 1954, Charleston just missed the killer storm, Hazel. The Grand Strand wasn't as lucky. Hurricane Hazel all but destroyed

Myrtle Beach. Hurricane Gracie on September 29, 1959, was severe, but luckily, hit at low tide. And then came September 21, 1989, and Hugo.

After the storm of 1911, Captain J.H. Devereaux, superintendent of government buildings, denied a report that he was hurt on Sullivan's Island during the storm. "I passed through the gale of 1854, the cyclone of 1885, the storm of 1893 and I am satisfied that the force, velocity and endurance of the storm of this week is greater than any of those, always remembering, however, the answer Parminio gave Alexander the Great, when the general asked what was the greatest pain he could suffer: The philosopher replied, 'the present pain, sir.' "

Hooey-BOY!
The Mystery of History

RESEARCHING HISTORY IS A BIT like unraveling a mystery. Like a good "whodunit," it is putting together scraps of isolated facts (sometimes found in the least likely places), which are then assembled and looked at as a whole. Sometimes this job is naturally intriguing. Reading diaries and letters, for instance, is an enjoyable way of getting a more incisive look into a person or a period of time. Most of the time, however, researching history is a tedious process of plodding through what is, frankly, boring information. Reading deeds, wills and early laws and statutes is about as thrilling as studying tombstone inscriptions.

But then, occasionally, one hits historical pay dirt. These are times when yours truly will spontaneously defile the quiet sanctity of the research library and yell out a loud, " Hooey-BOY! Look what I found!" I would like to share two such "hooey-boys" with you and how research solved two historical "mysteries."

Subject 1: The Church of the Holy Cross, Sullivan's Island. The mystery? The stained glass window behind the altar, which is a beautifully executed work of the crucifixion, dedicated to the memory of a woman named Ella Benjamin. Who was Ella Benjamin? The information was not in the church records. I knew only that the general time period for the stained glass was the 1880s when the original church was erected. And that is all I knew.

Not having the death records at hand since I was working at the Charleston Library Society, I turned to the census books. Perhaps Ella was a wealthy landowner who had taken part of her millions to commission the stained glass for the church? No luck. I found many people with the name Benjamin, but no Ella. I pored through countless book indexes regarding life in Charleston in the 1880s, looking for Ella Benjamin's name. Again no luck. After several hours of frustration, I gave up.

Then serendipity stepped in to lend a hand. Someone had apparently been doing research earlier at the table at which I was sitting, and had left behind a copy of the *Historical & Genealogical Magazine* produced by the South Carolina Historical Society in 1913. I picked up the book and began to casually leaf through it, when the book opened, almost like magic, to page 177. There, in a completely unrelated article on a family called Brisbane, was Ella Benjamin's name! This is what I learned.

Born Elvira Nicoll Benjamin on November 27, 1840, Ella was swimming on Sullivan's Island near the Grillage on August 14, 1884, when a child, a young boy, became caught in a current. A strong swimmer, she swam out and held him above water until help came and the boy was saved. Miss Benjamin, however, drowned.

My next move was to go to microfilm and read the August 15, 1884, *News & Courier*. Sure enough, there was the complete story, beginning with the line, "A tragic occurrence at Sullivan's Island yesterday afternoon illustrates anew the heroism and self-sacrifice of which woman is capable.

Between 2 and 3 o'clock in the afternoon a number of children went in bathing in front of Dr. Kinloch's house on Sullivan's Island. The spot has always been considered a dangerous one and it is said that several persons have been drowned near the place. Miss Ella Benjamin, a resident of Charleston, who was boarding at Mrs. Walker's, house, went in to bathe with the children. Julian Reid, a little son of Mr. Loughton R. Reid, was among the children . . . and the little fellow got beyond his depth and was in imminent danger of losing his life. Miss Benjamin at once saw the peril, and being a good swimmer went to his rescue. She reached the drowning child, caught him in her arms and held him above the waves for nearly fifteen minutes until a boat in which were two colored men came up.

The little boy was rescued by the colored men, who also made an attempt to rescue Miss Benjamin. The prolonged efforts to save the life of the child, however, had evidently exhausted her strength. She kept afloat until the little boy was safe, and then sank. Every effort was made to recover her body, but it was fully twenty minutes after the drowning when the search was successful. At the expiration of that time Miss Benjamin's body floated to the surface and was taken ashore. The body of the lady will be brought to the city to-day for Interment.

The article ended with the line, "in Miss Benjamin, once more woman has immortalized herself, and so added yet another bright page to the history of woman's love and devotion."

Hooey-BOY! Not only had I found Ella Benjamin, I'd found a connection with such poignancy it still sends shivers down my spine. The stained glass window depicted ultimate sacrifice—the sacrifice of Christ on the cross—united with the sacrifice of a young woman who gave her life to save another's. And nobody, at least to my knowledge, knew about this touching connection. I'd unlocked a secret that had long been lost and which was well worth remembering. That felt *good*.

Subject 2: Sullivan's Island in the late 1600s. The mystery? What happened to the island's original trees? My gut feeling was that, as a typical barrier island, the island must have originally had some sort of maritime forest. What happened to it? Conjecture is sometimes dangerous when translating history. One is left with assumptions and they may or may not be true. The trees could have been felled to build houses. They could have gone to build the first Fort Moultrie. They could have been destroyed by any number of hurricanes. Erosion could have taken them. I had no proof and, without such proof, I could not satisfy my question.

Then one day when I least expected it, right there in black-and-white was my answer. I was perusing the early statutes for the year 1700, looking up an entirely different subject, when I came across the law passed to make Sullivan's Island "more remarkable to mariners." I had skimmed this act before; it was the same act that called for the building of a brick watchtower, one of the island's first lighthouses. I had made the assumption that it was this tower that made the island more " remarkable" to offshore sailors.

How wrong I was. Upon reading the act in its entirety, I found that it also stated that until the watchtower was erected, "all the under-woods of the said Island, such other of standing and growing trees thereof, be cut down and cleared . . . and . . . only the remarkable trees standing thereon be left . . . in such form and figure as may most conduce to the better distinguishing of said Island."

Good grief! They'd cut down the forest on purpose! How could vessels tell which island marked the entrance of Charleston harbor? All they had to do was look for the island *without* any trees! *Hooey-BOY!* Did I let out a whoop and a holler when I found this!

For those of you who are thinking, "who cares?" You probably don't read early statutes, either. But I do. And I love the mystery in history as much as any Agatha Christie whodunit. Of course, the importance of these discoveries depends entirely on the subject at hand. But when history is often only a relation of one misconception after another, coming to an undisputed truth is a real charge. And when I find one? Hooey-BOY! Count on it. I'll let you know.

Bibliography

Agassiz, Elizabeth Carey. *Louis Agassiz, His Life & Correspondence.*
    Boston: Houghton Mifflin & Co., 1888.
Allen, Hervey. *Israfel, The Life & Times of Edgar Allan Poe.* New York:
    George H. Doran Company, 1927.
Audubon, Maria R. *Audubon and His Journals.* New York:
    Charles Scribner's Sons, 1899.
Bearss, Edwin C. *The First Two Fort Moultries.* U.S. National
    Park Service, 1968.
Brewster, Lawrence Fay. *Summer Migrations & Resorts of South Carolina
    Low-Country Planters.* Durham: Duke University Press, 1947.
Carroll, B. R. *Historical Collections of South Carolina, Volumes I and II.*
    New York: Harper & Brothers, 1836.
Catesby, Marc. *The Natural History of Carolina, Florida & the
    Bahama Islands.* London, 1731.
Childs, St. Julien Ravenel. *Malaria and Colonization in the Carolina
    Low Country, 1526-1696.* Baltimore: Johns Hopkins Press, 1940.
Crafts, William. "Sullivan's Island." Charleston, 1820.
Dalcho, Frederick. *An Historical Account of the Protestant Episcopal Church
    in South Carolina.* Charleston: E. Thayer, 1820.

Doubleday, Abner. *Reminiscences of Forts Sumter and Moultrie in 1860-61.* New York: Harper & Brothers, 1876.

Drayton, John. *A View of South-Carolina as Respects her Natural and Civil Concerns.* Charleston: W. P. Young, 1802.

Edgar, Walter B. and N. Louise Baily, eds. *Biographical Directory of the South Carolina House of Representatives, Volume II, Commons House of Assembly, 1692-1775.* Columbia: University of South Carolina Press, 1977.

Gilman, Caroline Howard. *Recollections of a Southern Matron.* New York: Harper & Brothers, 1838.

Gosse, Philip. *The History of Piracy.* New York: Tudor Publishing Company, 1934.

Hamer, Philip M., George Rogers, David R. Chesnutt and C. James Taylor, eds. *The Papers of Henry Laurens (1747-1778),* Vols. 1-13. Columbia: University of South Carolina Press, 1968-1991.

Harrison, T.P., ed. "Journal of a Voyage to Charleston in So. Carolina by Peletiah Webster in 1765." Charleston: South Carolina Historical Society, 1898.

Higgins, Robert W. "The Geographical Origins of Negro Slaves in Colonial South Carolina," *South Atlantic Quarterly* Volume 70 (1971).

Howe, Reverend George. *History of the Presbyterian Church in South Carolina.* Columbia. Duffie & Chapman, 1870.

Hudson, Charles. *The Juan Pardo Expeditions: Exploration of the Carolinas and Tennessee, 1566-68.* Washington: Smithsonian Institute Press, 1990.

Irving, Dr. John Beaufain. "Local Events & Incidences at Home." Charleston, 1850.

————*A Day on the Cooper River.* Louisa Cheves Stoney, ed. Columbia: The R.L. Bryan Company, 1969.

Johnson, John. *The Defense of Charleston Harbor.* Charleston: Walker, Evans & Cogswell, Co., 1890.

Jones, George Fenwick. "John Martin Boltzius' Trip to Charleston, October 1742." *South Carolina Historical Magazine* Volume 82, (1981).

Jordan, L.W., Robert Dukes, Jr. and Ted Rosengarten, eds. "A History of Storms on the South Carolina Coast." Charleston: South Carolina Sea Grant Consortium, 1985.

Lawson, John. *A Voyage to Carolina Containing the Exact Description and Natural History of that Country, &c.* London, 1709.

Leland, John G. *Stede Bonnet, Gentleman Pirate of the Carolina Coast.* Charleston: Charleston Reproductions, 1972.

"Letters of Thomas Pinckney to Harriott Pinckney." *South Carolina Historical Magazine* Volume 58 (1957).

Littlefield, Daniel C. *Rice and Slaves: Ethnicity and the Slave Trade in Colonial South Carolina.* Baton Rouge: Louisiana State University Press, 1981.

Ludlum, David M. *Early American Hurricanes, 1491-1825.* Boston, 1963.

McIver, Petrona Royall. *History of Mount Pleasant, South Carolina.* Mount Pleasant: Town of Mount Pleasant, 1960.

Mills, Robert. *Statistics of South Carolina, including a View of its Natural, Civil and Military History, General and Particular.* Charleston: Hurlbut and Lloyd, 1826.

Milling, Chapman J. *Red Carolinians.* Columbia: University of South Carolina Press, 1940.

Moultrie, William. *Memoirs of the American Revolution.* New York, 1802.

Palmer, Colin. "African Slave Trade: The Cruelest Commerce." *National Geographic Magazine* Volume 182, no. 3 (September 1992).

Petit, James Percival. *South Carolina and the Sea (Two Volumes).* Charleston: State Ports Authority, Maritime and Ports Activities Committee, 1976.

Porcher, Frederick Adolphus. "Memoirs of Frederick Adolphus Porcher." *South Carolina Historical Magazine* Volume 49 (1948).

Quinn, Arthur Hobson. *Edgar Allan Poe, A Critical Biography.* London & New York: Appleton-Century Company, 1941.

Ravenel, Edmund. *The Advantages of a Sea-Shore Residence in the Treatment of Certain Diseases, and the Therapeutic Employment of Sea-Water.* Charleston: Walker & James, 1850.

Riley, Edward M. "Historic Fort Moultrie in Charleston Harbor." *South Carolina Historical Magazine* Volume 51 (1950).

Reiger, George. *Wanderer on my Native Shore.* New York: Simon and Schuster, 1983.

Rivers, William James. *A Sketch of the History of South Carolina.* Charleston, 1874.

Rogers, George C. Jr. *Charleston in the Age of the Pinckneys.* Columbia: University of South Carolina Press, 1969.

Saint-Amand, Mary Scott. *A Balcony in Charleston: Letters of Caroline Howard Gilman.* Richmond: Garret and Massic, Inc., 1941.

Salley, Alexander S. "The Early English Settlers of South Carolina." Printed for The National Society of the Colonial Dames of America in the State of South Carolina, 1946.

————*Journals of the Commons House of Assembly of South Carolina.* Columbia: The State Company, 1940.

————*Journals of the Grand Council, August 25, 1671 - June 24, 1681.* Columbia: Historical Commission of South Carolina, 1907.

————*Narratives of Early Carolina 1650-1708.* New York: Charles Scribner's Sons, 1911.

Simms, William Gilmore. "A Glance at the Watering Places." *International Magazine of Literature, Art & Science.* August 1, 1851.

Smith, Henry A.M. "Old Charles Town and its Vicinity, Accabee and Wappoo Where Indigo were First Cultivated, with some Adjoining Places in Old St. Andrews Parish." *The South Carolina Historical and Genealogical Magazine* Volume 16 (1915).

Soltow, James H. "A Tale of Two Resorts: Two Centuries of Economic Development at the Seashore." *The Journal of the Economic and Business Historical Society* Volume 15 (1997).

Spence, E. Lee. *Shipwrecks of South Carolina & Georgia, 1521-1865.* Charleston: Sea Research Society/College of Charleston, 1985.

————*Treasures of the Confederate Coast: The "Real Rhett Butler" & Other Revelations.* Miami and Charleston: Narwhal Press, Inc., 1995.

Stoney, John Safford. "Recollections of John Safford Stoney, Confederate Surgeon." *South Carolina Historical Magazine* Volume 60 (1959).

Swanton, John R. *Indians of the Southeastern United States.* Washington: United States Government Printing Office, 1946.

————*Early History of the Creek Indians and Their Neighbors.* Washington: Smithsonian Institute, Bureau of Ethnology, United States Government Printing Office, 1922.

————*The Indian Tribes of North America.* Washington: United States Government Printing Office, 1953.

Wallace, David Duncan. *South Carolina: A Short History.* Chapel Hill: University of North Carolina Press, 1951.

Walsh, Richard. *Charleston's Sons of Liberty.* Columbia: University of South Carolina Press, 1959.

Waring, Joseph Ioor. *A History of Medicine in South Carolina, 1670-1825.* Columbia, 1964.

———*Medicine in Charleston, 1750-1775,* Charleston, 1935.